D1189751

AMERICAN EDUCATION

Its Men,

Ideas,

and

Institutions

Advisory Editor

Lawrence A. Cremin
Frederick A. P. Barnard Professor of Education
Teachers College, Columbia University

AMERICAN EDUCATION: *Its Men, Ideas, and Institutions*
presents selected works of thought and scholarship that have
long been out of print or otherwise unavailable. Inevitably, such
works will include particular ideas and doctrines that have been
outmoded or superseded by more recent research. Nevertheless,
all retain their place in the literature, having influenced educational thought and practice in their own time and having provided
the basis for subsequent scholarship.

THE MONTESSORI METHOD

AND

THE AMERICAN SCHOOL

BY

FLORENCE ELIZABETH WARD

ARNO PRESS & THE NEW YORK TIMES
*New York * 1971*

Reprint Edition 1971 by Arno Press Inc.

Reprinted from a copy in
  The University of Illinois Library

American Education:
  Its Men, Ideas, and Institutions - Series II
ISBN for complete set: 0-405-03600-0
See last pages of this volume for titles.

Manufactured in the United States of America

Library of Congress Cataloging in Publication Data

Ward, Florence Elizabeth.
    The Montessori method and the American school.
    (American education: its men, ideas, and
institutions. Series II)
    Bibliography: p.
    1. Montessori method of education. I. Title.
II. Series.
LB775.M8W3 1971   372.1'3   70-165744
ISBN 0-405-03722-8

THE MONTESSORI METHOD
AND THE AMERICAN SCHOOL

MARIA MONTESSORI.

THE MONTESSORI METHOD

AND

THE AMERICAN SCHOOL

BY

FLORENCE ELIZABETH WARD

PROFESSOR OF KINDERGARTEN EDUCATION
IOWA STATE TEACHERS COLLEGE

New York

THE MACMILLAN COMPANY

1913

THE MACMILLAN COMPANY
NEW YORK · BOSTON · CHICAGO · DALLAS
ATLANTA · SAN FRANCISCO

MACMILLAN & CO., LIMITED
LONDON · BOMBAY · CALCUTTA
MELBOURNE

THE MACMILLAN CO. OF CANADA, LTD.
TORONTO

Norwood Press
J. S. Cushing Co. — Berwick & Smith Co.
Norwood, Mass., U.S.A.

This Book

IS OFFERED AS A TOKEN OF APPRECIATION

TO

THE LARGE—HEARTED, BROAD—MINDED

PHYSICIAN AND TEACHER

IN MY COPY OF WHOSE EPOCH—MAKING BOOK

APPEARS THE FOLLOWING

Alla cara Signorina Florence E. Ward — che credo amica di questa opera d' educazione — con affetto

Maria Montessori

Roma — Maggio 1912

PREFACE

THE Montessori Method has been given so much publicity by the American press that its peculiarities have become quite generally known, and one who attempts to describe them further is in danger of repetition. It is my aim, however, simply to offer to those who have a practical interest in its intimate details some of the impressions received through an investigation of the Method at first hand, as well as some results of experiments made among children with whom I work daily at the Iowa State Teachers College.

The talks herein published are the substance of discussions conducted with classes, following my return from Rome. It is not their purpose to crystallize attention upon some one feature of the equipment or upon some one element of the method, but rather to promote the study of the principles underlying the entire equipment and the entire method.

All pedagogical history proves that reforms in education develop slowly. It would be a curious anomaly if the Children's House did not conform to this law of evolution. Its best friends are those who willingly submit it to the comparisons possible because of work done in the exceptionally good home, good kindergarten and good primary school of to-day, and to the tests that the psychological laboratories are urging for all educational procedure.

As in any earnest study one should turn at once to original sources, so a student of this method should take as a basic text Dr. Montessori's own book, "The Montessori Method." (Frederick A. Stokes Co., New York.) The material herein offered does not claim to be a complete interpretation of the principles and practices of Dr. Montessori, but a supplementary discussion of these and their application to our American problems.

If, as the book goes out, it prompts questions which make clearer my own understanding, one purpose will have been fulfilled. If other students of the Method, in home or school, are led to clearer insight, another purpose will have been realized.

In arranging these talks for publication, conferences with Miss Alma L. Binzel, Dr. Effie McCollum Jones, Professor Chauncey P. Colegrove, and Professor Wilbur H. Bender have been most helpful. Acknowledgment is also due to Mr. James M. Pierce, President of the House of Childhood, 200 Fifth Avenue, New York, for many photographs.

The following publishers have graciously permitted the use of copyrighted material: Frederick A. Stokes Co., World Book Co., D. Appleton & Co., Henry Holt & Co., Ginn & Co., Century Co., Harper & Bros., The A. S. Barnes Co., Sigma Publishing Co., David McKay, Teachers College, Columbia University, and the University of Chicago.

FLORENCE ELIZABETH WARD.

INTRODUCTORY REMARKS

INTEREST in the Montessori Method brought many letters of inquiry to The Iowa State Teachers College, and prompted the provision for a series of discussions on this subject at the Summer Session of 1912.

Being the one appointed to lead these discussions, and knowing little of the Method except what had been gleaned from popularly written magazine articles, I decided to go to Rome, on leave of absence, to gain what insight I could at the fountainhead. So, accompanied by another kindergartner bent on the same mission, I sailed for Europe in the early spring.

En route we stopped at Tarrytown, New York, where Miss Anne E. George, Dr. Montessori's first American pupil, was conducting a real Montessori school. Miss George was enthusiastic over the results of her experiments with Montessori ideas and materials among the favored children of the American rich. She had worked for eight months in the schools of Rome, dealing largely with children of the street who look after themselves from the time they can walk. She told of her delight in discovering that these two types of children, so different in nationality and social opportunity, had fundamentally the same instincts, impulses and desires, and that the Tarrytown children responded as delightfully to the Montessori environment as did the Italian children of the slums. (Miss George has since established a permanent Montessori school in Washington. She is probably, at this time, the best-informed and most skillful American exponent of the method.)

Arriving in Boston, we went to Cambridge for a conference with Professor Henry W. Holmes, who wrote the introduction to the American edition of Dr. Montessori's book. Professor Holmes is one of the few men identified with great universities who has made a thorough study of Froebelian philosophy, and his comparisons of the Casa dei Bambini and the Kindergarten were most illuminating.

We spent one profitable afternoon visiting the Massachusetts School for the Feeble-minded at Waverly, where the materials developed by Dr. Edward Seguin, the famous French specialist for defectives, are in use. As is well known, Dr. Montessori has adapted these materials for the training of normal children. It may be of interest to note here that Dr. Seguin came to America in 1850, that for many years, until his death, he was active in promoting scientific methods for the treatment of defective children, and that Mrs. Seguin still carries forward the work of her illustrious husband in a private school at East Orange, New Jersey. The Superintendent of the Waverly institution, Dr. Walter S. Fernald, a man of clear vision and broad sympathy in his work, showed us the Seguin materials and explained their practical, daily use in his remarkable school.

Through the courtesy of the Frederick A. Stokes Publishing Company, we received on shipboard one of the first copies of the English translation of Dr. Montessori's book as it came from the press. This book we read with eagerness, and by the time we had reached Naples its pages were well worn from lending, as many passengers desired a peep into the book whose publication had been looked for with keen anticipation by

American students of child life. It proved delightful reading, showing as it did the sympathetic, womanly spirit of the author as well as her fine intellectual insight. It gave us a general exposition of the method, the needs which called it into existence, the principles upon which it was based, and the results realized in actual practice.

On arriving in Rome, we found ourselves surrounded by Americans whose purpose was the same as our own, but we soon realized that one's presence there did not insure illumination on the subject of the Montessori method. No training courses were being offered for teachers ; the Dottoressa was difficult of access ; her schools were not open to the public; and those who won entrance into her laboratory and her confidence counted themselves fortunate. She was no respecter of persons in the matter of those she received. The college professor, accustomed to recognition ; the school superintendent, whose word is law ; the zealous, not-to-be-thwarted kindergartner and primary teacher ; to say nothing of the purposeful settlement worker ; the persistent reporter ; and the affable photographer, — all came to a sudden halt at the threshold of this quiet, unassuming originator. With many desiring to see her, she went serenely on, testing her theories with groups of children, apparently caring little for worldly recognition or financial gain.

Sometimes days passed before one could arrange for an interview. In this waiting period, expectancy changed to disappointment, and irritation to chagrin. But as it is human nature to strive for the thing most difficult to obtain, perseverance knew no bounds and the belated message which opened doors to the scene of action was most welcome. Once admitted, one was treated with the greatest cordiality. "I am willing to see those who are here in search of truth," said Dr. Montessori, "but many come out of curiosity or with a passion for the new and the unusual. I cannot meet these purloiners of time. If I saw all callers and answered all letters, I should have no time for experiment and study, and my system is not yet completed."

I remember with pleasure my first conference with Dr. Montessori. Accustomed to associate eccentricity with genius, I confess to a happy disappointment. Her attractive home is but a suitable setting for this gracious, queenly woman, whose charm of manner and womanly poise make her a joy to look upon. Becomingly gowned and free from affectation, she illustrates the fact that there is no necessary antagonism between brilliancy of mind and attractiveness of person.

To say that she answers all questions, or that her system solves all pedagogical problems, as some enthusiasts do, is manifestly absurd. The Dottoressa herself makes no such sweeping claim. That she points the way toward a marked advance along some lines of reform in early education, there is little chance for doubt. Like many others, I went to Rome with some question as to whether the peculiar personal development of educational theories might not have been unduly exploited by seekers of magazine sensation. I came away with the conviction that certain influences of the Casa dei Bambini will be distinct and permanent contributions to the enrichment of child life.

TABLE OF CONTENTS

ILLUSTRATIONS

THE MONTESSORI METHOD
AND THE AMERICAN SCHOOL

THE MONTESSORI METHOD AND THE AMERICAN SCHOOL

CHAPTER I

THE EVOLUTION OF THE METHOD

An Italian physician and teacher has worked out a plan for directing the activities of little children —̇ a plan so unusual that her modest schools in Rome have attracted the attention of educators on two continents, provoked universal newspaper and magazine comment and caused the migration to Rome of many a teacher, psychologist and social worker, some representing colleges, universities and even governments in official capacity.

This new method, denounced by some as a fad, extolled by others as a solution of all our pedagogical problems, has been discovered before its completion, and its quiet, unassuming originator, Doctor Maria Montessori, reluctantly finds herself the center of a storm of question, adulation and criticism.

The general interest in this method, which began to manifest itself in America a few years ago, has been considerably heightened by the appearance of an English translation of Doctor Montessori's Educational Treatise, and by the organization of an American corporation, known as the House of Childhood, for the manufacture and distribution of her didactic materials.

Thus in possession of both the book and the equipment, American students of child life are considering what features are practical for our uses. They are comparing the old with the new, and challenging the new to prove its right to a place in our educational practice.

The present widespread discussion of Montessori ideas, significant of the restlessness and discontent with existing school conditions, is in the line of progress, for though we may justly claim to maintain in America the best system of public kindergarten and primary schools in the world, we are not satisfied with present attainments, nor do we assume that the final word has been spoken with reference to child training. Indeed, the attention accorded this method is but another illustration of America's well-known hospitality toward helpful ideas, from whatever source.

Some of the most valuable elements of our educational work are importations. The contribution of the kindergarten made by Germany has enriched the American child's life beyond measure, and it is a suggestive fact that the successful American kindergarten, adapted and adopted under present century enlightenment to meet the needs of American temperament, social environment and national ideals, is a far better exemplification of Froebelian philosophy than the kindergartens of the Fatherland. May it not legitimately follow that whatever in the Montessori Method is fundamental, and hence applicable to universal child nature, may because of our liberal and democratic spirit be worked out even more ideally here than in Italy?

The story of the beginning and growth of the Montessori Method is an interesting one. It tells how a woman's mind, which had been highly trained for one purpose, was seized by quite another idea and drawn into quite another field of activity, and how the way was made plain for this unexpected pioneering by a combination of circumstances so fortuitous as to seem almost to belong to a romantic age rather than to our scientific century.

A notion prevails that the teacher is born, not made; that from early childhood the future pedagogue gathers her playmates about her and conducts an imaginary school. Here Maria Montessori breaks with tradition. It was the dream of her life to become a physician, and with energy and high spirit she turned her unusually gifted personality in that direction. It was no light thing in Italy for a young woman to secure the training she sought. Social prejudice, intellectual bigotry and professional jealousies barred her way, but with characteristic persistence she reached her goal and was the first woman to receive the degree of Doctor of Medicine at the University of Rome, where she later conducted lecture courses in pedagogical anthropology.[1]

Her success as a student was brilliant enough to have promised for her a conspicuous future as a physician. Yet it was this very medical training which served as a means to lead her into the educational field. Her first step in that direction was taken when as an Assistant Doctor at the Psychiatric Clinic of the University of Rome she frequently visited the slums and insane hospitals for suitable subjects.

[1] Pedagogical Anthropology. Montessori. Frederick A. Stokes Co.

A keen interest in children's diseases, especially those of defectives, took possession of this noble woman. She became intensely interested in the social problems of the poor. One who has not visited the poverty-stricken sections of Rome can have little conception of the conditions there, where want and depravity produce many abnormal children, some functionally defective, others unawakened and backward. Doctor Montessori attacked this situation with all her instinctive maternal sympathy, and soon came out with the assertion that idiocy was not alone the problem of the physician, but of the teacher as well; that pedagogy more than medicine could improve conditions.[1]

The outgrowth of her agitation of this theory was the establishment of the State Orthophrenic School, of which she became head. Here she not only trained teachers in special methods of dealing with the feeble minded, but taught the children herself, often working from eight in the morning until seven at night, almost without intermission. "These two years of practice," says Dr. Montessori, "are my first and indeed my true degree in pedagogy."

"Every new system bears the stamp of a personality; the element is strongly marked in this particular case by reason of the high enthusiasm of the author, and energy instinct as it were with the maternal passion, the passion for saving and upbuilding, which makes women the great conservative force in society. In the case of Dr. Montessori, this energy has been directed by prolonged training in the sciences that relate to human life, and vitalized by practical experience in their application to needy and defective children. In brief, her method is the outcome of genius, training,

[1] "An Educational Wonder Worker." McClure's, May 1911.

and experience. This combination of qualities is not only certain from the testimony of her associates, but it is borne out by the first chapter of her book, which, although bearing the caption 'Critical Considerations,' is more truly a revelation of her own sympathetic nature and a record of reflections excited by the unnatural restraints placed upon children whom she observed." [1]

Doctor Montessori wrote and lectured extensively, urging scientific and corrective measures for this neglected class of children. For light upon the subject, she turned to Itard, the famous French physician, who, she asserts, made the first practical attempts at experimental psychology. She also studied his disciple, Seguin, many of whose materials she has modified and adapted in her system. [2] She investigated these theories with vigor, translating into Italian the books of these famous French specialists, and visiting Paris and London for purposes of research.

"Having through actual experience justified my faith in Seguin's method, I withdrew from active work among deficients, and began a more thorough study of the works of Itard and Seguin. I felt the need of meditation. I did a thing which I had not done before, and which perhaps few students have been willing to do, — I translated into Italian and copied out with my own hand the writings of these men, from beginning to end, making for myself books as the old Benedictines used to do before the diffusion of printing." [3]

Through years of untiring devotion to this work, to which she brought not only the experience of a practicing physician, but also the patient concentration of a student,

[1] The Montessori System of Education. United States Bureau of Education. Bulletin 1912, No. 17.

[2] Idiocy and its Treatment by the Physiological Method. Seguin.

[3] The Montessori Method, p. 41.

she evolved a plan of teaching, by which abnormal children were brought up to grade, passing the usual tests of normal children of the same age.

To prove the efficiency of her method, she asked to have these children admitted to the municipal schools of Rome. The permission was reluctantly granted. When the teachers saw the advancement of these defectives, they said, "This is a miracle." The Dottoressa replied that if they, by the use of scientific methods, would give the children under their charge as fair a chance, her success would not seem a miracle; for normal children, having no handicap, would make proportionally an even greater advance.

Doctor Montessori later withdrew from the active work of teaching defectives, and reëntered the University of Rome, where her grasp of philosophical and scientific subjects made her a dreaded opponent in argument or debate among her classmen.

The more she considered her methods, the more she was convinced that they were broad enough to apply to all classes of children, normal as well as abnormal.

"From the very beginning of my work with deficient children (1898 to 1900) I felt that the methods which I used had in them nothing peculiarly limited to the instruction of idiots. I believed that they contained educational principles more rational than those in use, so much more so, indeed, that through their means an inferior mentality would be able to grow and develop. This feeling, so deep as to be in the nature of an intuition, became my controlling idea after I had left the school for deficients, and, little by little, I became convinced that similar methods applied to normal children would develop or set free their personality in a marvellous and surprising way." [1]

[1] The Montessori Method, pp. 32–33.

An almost capricious favor of circumstance brought an agency to hand which provided opportunity and material for Doctor Montessori to test her belief. An organization called the Roman Association for Good Building owned many tenements in the Quarter of San Lorenzo, and in other poor and neglected districts. It was decided to rebuild some of these, converting them into modern apartments with light, air and sanitation, and providing modern schoolrooms within the buildings — a plan prompted by the combined motives of commercial enterprise and social uplift.

Doctor Montessori was invited to take charge of these schools, and was offered a free hand as to method, equipment and organization. Immediately she saw the social significance and educational possibilities of such a scheme and accepted the commission, establishing the first school in Via dei Masi, January, 1907, and christening it with the happy name of Casa dei Bambini, or Children's House. Others were started soon after, and it is in these much talked of schools that Doctor Montessori has demonstrated, to her own satisfaction and that of thousands of visitors, the power of a few well-known but often neglected principles governing child life.

Such a rare opportunity for the testing of theories comes to but few educators. Given full charge of small groups of children with the privilege of providing for them ideal physical and social environment, with admission requirements which eliminated objectionable conditions and preserved for each child that personal liberty upon which the method was based, she watched without hindrance the demonstration of her theories.

CASA DEI BAMBINI.

Children were admitted between the ages of three and seven. While there was no tuition charged, parents availing themselves of the privileges of the school pledged the following:

"(a) To send their children to the 'Children's House' at the appointed time, clean in body and clothing, and provided with a suitable apron.

" (b) To show the greatest respect and deference toward the Directress and toward all persons connected with the 'Children's House,' and to coöperate with the Directress herself in the education of the children. Once a week, at least, the mothers may talk with the Directress, giving her information concerning the home life of the child, and receiving helpful advice from her.

" There shall be expelled from the 'Children's House':

" (a) Those children who present themselves unwashed, or in soiled clothing.

" (b) Those who show themselves to be incorrigible.

" (c) Those whose parents fail in respect to the persons connected with the 'Children's House' or who destroy through bad conduct the educational work of the institution." [1]

Doctor Montessori has now given up her official relations with the Good Building Association. The only school under her personal charge is the Cloister School conducted by the Franciscan Missionary Nuns in Via Giusti. This is her laboratory and the best school of its kind in Rome, giving the truest interpretation of the Dottoressa's ideals.

The statement is made by critics that only a teacher of peculiar skill, perhaps a Montessori herself, with a selected group of children could secure desirable results from this method. One finds on investigation, however, that there are a number of fairly good schools in widely

[1] The Montessori Method, pp. 70–71.

THE FOUNTAIN. THE CLOISTER SCHOOL.

Water is a fascinating play medium that has long been used. It is, unfortunately, a tabooed one for some children.

differing quarters of Rome. Indeed, the schools established in the slums several years ago reach now to the other extreme of the social stratum. In the Casa dei Bambini on Pincian Hill one sees the carefully reared scions of the exclusive aristocracy using the didactic materials and receiving the social training provided for the children of the Ghetto at the Municipal School of St. Angelo in Pescheria, a most poverty-stricken quarter. Between these extremes there are such schools as the one in Via Giusti. That Doctor Montessori's method has merit is demonstrated by the fact that with these various types of children, despite their differences in heredity, home environment and early training, it gains a measure of success; and this when the teachers, from the scholarly, scientific Montessori to the cloistered white-robed Sisters, show almost an equal range of characteristics and personality.

Doctor Montessori's work is not, however, meant to end with beginners. She has in her own home, in the neighborhood of the Piazza del Popolo, a class for children beyond the age of six, to which few visitors are admitted and in which she is testing plans for carrying forward her principles into the work of the grades, hoping to offer an advance and simplification along that line.

She proves on acquaintance to be an untiring seeker after truth. Personal recognition, and especially sensational notoriety, are apparently farthest from her desire. She makes no sweeping claims of originality, but gives full credit to other workers in the same field.

"Here lies the significance of my pedagogical experiment in the 'Children's Houses.' It represents the results of a series of trials made by me, in the education of young children, with methods already used with deficients. My work has not been in any way an application, pure and simple, of the methods of Seguin to young children, as any one who will consult the works of the author will readily see. But it is none the less true that, underlying these two years of trial, there is a basis of experiment which goes back to the days of the French Revolution and which represents the earnest work of the lives of Itard and Seguin." [1]

Efforts have been made to establish schools based on the Montessori idea in Switzerland, France, England and other countries. Perhaps the latest and most significant development is the organization of a Montessori Educational Association in Washington (the outgrowth of Miss George's School) for the propagation of Montessori ideals in America. Officers and patrons of this organization are men and women whose names add stability to the movement. Doctor Montessori's training class for teachers, recently conducted in Rome, was attended by a number of Americans well known in educational work.

[1] The Montessori Method, p. 45.

CHAPTER II

THE strait-laced educator with traditional notions as to what a school should be in outward appearance and inner aim has in store a distinct sense of shock when he, with the necessary credentials in hand, first sets foot inside the Casa dei Bambini.

He may arrive between ten and eleven in the morning and find himself within a large and airy room, looking out upon an open court with generous spaces for gardens and games. He will be apt to see some thirty children between the ages of three and six, very much alive, and doing to all appearances exactly as they please, quite independent of each other and quite unconscious of the appearance of a visitor, so absorbed are they in their various interests. Perhaps a dozen different activities are going on at once, the children moving about without restraint, adjusting the small, light-weight tables and chairs to suit the convenience of the moment.

There seems at first to be no teacher present with these self-contained, happy children, but one is there within easy reach, though without rostrum or desk from which to reign. She goes quietly about, giving a suggestion here or a bit of instruction there. Sometimes she is the center of a group of expectant, upturned faces, but oftener she deals with the individual child.

Our visitor, observing all this at a glance, may feel quite justified in declaring that, while this is an interesting place as one of the novel sights of modern Rome, it is not a school at all, as it violates every principle of formal school organization. There are no rows of children waiting to respond to the beck and call of the teacher. There are no classes engaged in prescribed occupations. The only groups are the natural ones formed by the children themselves because of their mutual tastes and present interest. There is not that unnatural quiet of suppressed, inactive children so often felt in a schoolroom, although the busy hum of gentle voices has in it no confusion or disorder. And as the day advances, our visitor may feel that this interesting place is even less like a school and more difficult to understand. The only way that he will be able to put himself into a sympathetic and intelligent attitude toward this strange institution will be to catch the newer idea of what constitutes a school. If its purpose is to furnish an environment where children may grow toward the highest self-realization while they are being prepared for social life, and if the only organization desired is that which shall contribute to such an end, then, putting prejudice and tradition aside, he may be able to see how this Children's House is in a measure fulfilling such a mission; and following the work through an entire day, he will see, too, that back of this apparent lack of organization there is order and purpose.

It will be illuminating for our observer to keep in mind some of the underlying ideas of the method, such as the following:

"(1) If a new and scientific pedagogy is to arise from the study of the individual, such study must occupy itself with the observation of free children."

"(2) He who experiments must, while doing so, divest himself of every preconception."

"(3) Life acts of itself, and to divine its secrets or direct its activity it is necessary to observe without intervening." — MONTESSORI.

The Montessori school covers a long day, but one so broken by household activities, luncheon, nap and rest period, free play and gardening, that it calls for but two and one half hours of actual school work.

The children arrive early and are soon industriously carrying on the first activity of the day, the toilet making, a feature particularly desirable among the class of children found in the poorer districts. The low washstands with their complete equipment of miniature bowl, pitcher, and other conveniences, are so adapted to the children's needs that they wash their faces and hands, brush their hair, care for their teeth and nails, and come out of the process bright and shining with an air of pride and the self-respect of the well-groomed.

The aprons, distinguished by embroidered names, are kept at the school, the older children helping the younger ones to put on this finishing touch, thus often covering a multitude of shortcomings and placing all on an equal footing as far as appearances are concerned.

The next bit of procedure is the inspection of the schoolroom by the children. Armed with pans, and little brooms, they vigorously attack every corner where dirt might be found hiding, and with absorbed interest and housewifely precision sweep and fold their rugs, arrange

THE OLDER CHILDREN HELP THE YOUNGER ONES.

the furnishings of the room, give water to the thirsty plants, and put snugly into cupboards every stray bit of didactic material. The joy with which they enter into real work with real results is indeed a pleasing sight.

When this is done, they seat themselves in their comfortable chairs before the small worktables. The directress calls attention to correct ways of sitting, rising and standing, gives exercises in politeness, and remarks upon the satisfaction one feels in having everything clean and in order. Then follows a happy morning talk with the exchange of ideas and interests between directress and pupils. After this comes the morning prayer and hymn.

During this time the little tables are arranged in orderly fashion, giving the appearance of the ordinary schoolroom. But now the time has come for the object lessons and sense games, and the children begin to move about with the greatest freedom and initiative, going to the low, convenient cupboards for the didactic materials in the use of which these schools are so unusual.

The chairs and tables are moved to any part of the room or courtyard which best suits the comfort of the children. Green rugs are thrown down by those who wish to work upon the floor. There is no apparent restraint, yet there is no disorder. This work is varied, yet there is no confusion. Children go freely about the room and courtyard, taking materials from the cupboards and putting them away again when they wish to change their occupation. One watches with absorbed attention, not so much because of the strange toys these children

c

are using as because of their purposeful, happy enjoyment of them and their apparent indifference to the presence of the directress.

The chests of drawers, about the size of a doll's dresser, containing cloths of different textures, are brought forth, and one child has a self-imposed bandage placed over his bright eyes, so that the sensitive finger tips may better decide whether the squares of cloth are of silk, linen, velvet or wool. The delicate fingers seem to like the contact, for later, with eyes tightly closed, the child may be seen smoothing a visitor's shirt waist and glove.

A little girl unconsciously cultivates the retentive muscular memory by the use of a polished wooden block which she has taken from the cupboard. This block contains cylindrical insets of different sizes. These are removed from the solid block, placed in a promiscuous pile and fitted into the holes to which they belong. As the large cylinder will not go into the small hole, or the tall one into the shallow hole, the child, through the sense of touch, finally places each in its snug socket and settles back with an air of satisfaction.

Instead of leaving this finished task, as one might expect, she looks about contentedly for a few moments and then begins all over again, taking the cylinders out and mixing them up on the table; the childish passion for arranging things in rows, and the pleasure of being able to see and correct one's mistakes, furnishing the incentive.

One group is working most industriously. Each has a light embroidery frame to which has been attached,

on either side, strips of cloth or leather with suitable
fastenings.   A chubby boy is vigorously buttoning the
leather pieces together.   A miss of three is pushing

SHOE BUTTONS.   LACINGS.

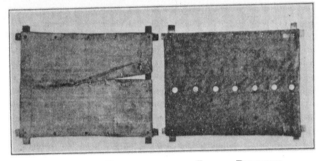

HOOKS AND EYES.   LARGE BUTTONS.

pearl buttons through firm buttonholes to join two
pieces of linen.   The third of the trio, a girl some months
older, is tying her pieces of cloth together with strips of
ribbon, spreading out the bows and ends in a way that
would do credit to a grown-up.   Other small fingers are
gaining in cunning by feeling the edges of geometric
insets, circular, square and oblong.   These, like the
cylinders, fit perfectly into the spaces provided for them,

making an exercise by which a child may detect and overcome his own errors.

Children who have dropped down upon the rugs with their blocks are lost to all other things. It is evident

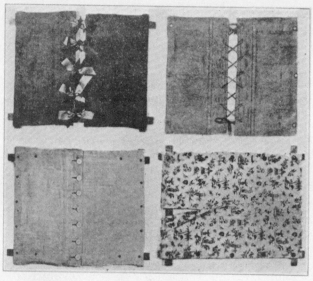

THE FRAMES.

Each frame embodies some process which helps the child to become independent in dressing himself.

at a glance that these blocks are not for creative building exercises, but to develop the sense perception of size, proportion and number. One child builds up the long stair, and its slender rods of red and blue, which emphasize the distinction between long and short, form steps of these bright colors. Another contentedly shoves together the thick and thin blocks of the broad stair which, when the ten parts are correctly placed, form complete and even steps of graduated prisms.

The pink tower is built to its highest point. Each of these three exercises is self-corrective, which accounts for the children's long-continued enjoyment of them.

A group is formed about a table for an absorbing game in matching colors with many bobbins of bright silk threads. The child's love of scribbling is gratified by exercises consisting of free strokes of large pencils, filling in circles, squares and triangles in geometric design — an unconscious preparation for writing. Some are arranging words and phrases with the pink consonants and blue vowels of the alphabet, the words standing out brightly on the green rug.

In all these activities the teacher follows rather than leads the children, and except for an occasional bit of assistance or advice, she is not much in evidence. Sometimes she gathers a small company of children about her for a group exercise, but there seems to be no occasion for her to raise her voice above a quiet, composed tone or to command the attention of the children.

To observe so many children with such a degree of self-mastery and composure is provocative of thought. Just what is the secret of this atmosphere of calm ? Is it the didactic material, the teacher's personality or the Italian temperament ?   Are the children old beyond their years and are they losing something of their babyhood ? They do not seem to be ; they are all quite childishly joyous and happy ; and while the teacher is alert, intelligent and sympathetic, it cannot be her influence alone. Are these self-contained, energetic little beings a bit unsocial ? Except for an occasional group of dark heads seen together, each child works by himself.

PREPARING THE TABLES FOR LUNCHEON.

It is not long, however, before one is convinced that the child's love of comradeship and play are not lost sight of, as evidenced by the buoyancy and freedom of both children and directress during the game period in the open courtyard. A chord is struck on the piano. Instantly these much-absorbed, silent and apparently self-centered little mortals briskly put away their materials in anticipation of the jolly coöperative march, the games and the luncheon which are to follow. Not every one comes to the circle on the instant. A few who have not quite finished or have just reached an interesting climax continue in their work, only glancing up occasionally to smile or chuckle at the frolics of the others. These children later join the playing group without comment from the directress.

At luncheon time, all come in wide awake and refreshed. The simple meal is served by little waiters and waitresses appointed for the day, who, without accident, carry tureens of soup and pitchers of water with skill and ease. Later, when the luncheon is over, an industrious band gathers up and washes the dishes, sorts and puts away the silver, sweeps and dusts the room, all after the manner of very good housekeepers.

Great delight is shown by the children in this part of the day's program. They eagerly watch the bulletin which announces from day to day the names of those appointed to act as helpers. It is because of Doctor Montessori's belief that the child hungers for reality and for real purposeful activity that she puts into his hands these tools for the household processes. Hence, the purpose of these exercises is not primarily to pre-

pare children for service to their elders, but for an aid
to physical and moral development.

The children are given only those things to do which
they have gained the power to accomplish through such
definite exercises as moving furnishings silently, mount-
ing and descending stairs without touching a railing,
sitting, standing, bowing, and greeting each other
correctly.

The afternoon is occupied with games, hand work,
gymnastics and gardening, and though the day is long,
the luncheon and rest period give the relaxation and
nourishment needed, and there is apparently no undue
weariness or nervous strain.

A day's program follows :

"Opening at nine o'clock — Closing at four o'clock.

9–10.   Entrance. Greeting. Inspection as to personal
             cleanliness. Exercises of practical life; helping
             one another to take off and put on the aprons.
             Going over the room to see that everything is
             dusted and in order. Language: Conversation
             period: Children give an account of the events
             of the day before. Religious exercises.

10–11.   Intellectual exercises. Objective lessons interrupted
             by short rest periods. Nomenclature. Sense
             exercises.

11–11 : 30. Simple gymnastics: Ordinary movements done
             gracefully, normal position of the body, walking,
             marching in line, salutations, movements for
             attention, placing of objects gracefully.

11 : 30–12. Luncheon: Short prayer.

12–1.   Free games.

LUNCHEON TIME.

1–2.   Directed games, if possible, in the open air. During this period the older children in turn go through with the exercises of practical life, cleaning the room, dusting, putting the material in order. General inspection for cleanliness: Conversation.

2–3.   Manual work. Clay modeling, design, etc.

3–4.   Collective gymnastics and songs, if possible in the open air. Exercises to develop forethought: Visiting and caring for the plants and animals." [1]

One who is familiar with the ideals of Colonel Francis W. Parker, our American pioneer in the movement for school socialization, as illustrated some years ago at the Cook County Normal, Chicago, is reminded of these ideals in observing Montessori's procedure. Colonel Parker says:

"A school is a community; community life is indispensable to mental and moral growth. If the act of an individual in any way hinders the best work of the community, he is in the wrong. The highest duty of the individual is to contribute all in his power to the best good of all. This principle is the sure guide to all rules and regulations of a school. How much noise shall there be in the school? Just enough to assist each and all to do their best work. How quiet shall it be? Just quiet enough to assist each and all to do their best work. How much whispering? What shall be the rules for coming in and going out? For punctuality? Every rule of a school, in order that it may be of educative influence and be felt to be right by each pupil, consists in carrying out this motto — 'Everything to help and nothing to hinder.' The first essential to true manhood is to feel the dignity of life, and that dignity comes from a sense of responsibility for the conduct of others.

There is but one test, one genuine test, of a school, which may be

[1] The Montessori Method, pp. 119–120.

explained by two questions : First, is every individual in this school doing educative work in the most economical way? Second, is that work the best for the whole, and at the same time the best for each individual? If the answer to these questions is in the affirmative in regard to any school, then it can be said to be in order. The perfect ideal of order is that each and every minute shall be filled with that work which best assists each and all in growth and development." [1]

[1] From Parker's Talks on Pedagogics, copyright 1894, The A. S. Barnes Company, publishers.

CHAPTER III

If Doctor Montessori had adapted no didactic material, if she had developed no unusual notions as to sense training or introduced no gymnastic apparatus for muscular coördination, she would still be entitled to a place among educational leaders. Her title to this eminence would come from the fact that she has so emphatically urged the necessity for the freedom of the child, and that she has so successfully demonstrated in her schools the possibilities of growth through an application of this principle, that educators are associating the words "freedom" and "the child" in their discussion of the Montessori Method in a way to center interest upon, and bring enlightenment into, the discussion of the most fundamental problem of American education.

This problem is, — how to develop thinking, executive, socialized individuals who will bring to their citizenship all of their powers and talents awakened, stimulated and trained to the highest realization. Such a development of poise and power must come in large measure through the school life.

Fundamental to all Doctor Montessori's plans for the child, is her reverence for his personality. She believes that this, his most sacred gift, can develop only in an atmosphere of freedom, not only the freedom of fresh air, sunshine, comfortable clothing, good food and broad open spaces, all of which she insists upon, but that far more vital freedom, the freedom from invasion by adult personalities. Believing that environment, while it cannot create character, can do much to advance or hinder its development, she puts within the child's reach that which tends to awaken and stimulate his powers and to satisfy his desire for creative effort, then she leaves him to himself, confident that, thus untrammeled, his individuality will assert itself in a normal growth.

"To stimulate life, — leaving it then free to develop, to unfold, — herein lies the first task of the educator. In such a delicate task, a great art must suggest the moment, and limit the intervention, in order that we shall arouse no perturbation, cause no deviation, but rather that we shall help the soul which is coming into the fullness of life, and which shall live from its own forces." [1]

The only limitation she places about the child is the collective interest. She insists upon the need for checking whatever interferes with others or tends toward rudeness, "but all the rest, — every manifestation having a useful scope whatever it may be or under whatever form expressed must not only be permitted but encouraged."

Believing that the child should develop social virtues by personal contact with social problems, the school in her hands becomes a microcosm of the normal social community, wherein the child confronts and solves for himself real problems. Since the highest ideal of social

[1] The Montessori Method, p. 115.

THE RACE DOWN THE BROAD WALK AFTER A BUSY MORNING.
Casa dei Bambini, Pincian Hill.

organization is self-direction in the use of liberty under law, Montessori insists that the only legitimate discipline is that which leads the child to control himself. Instead of annihilating the will, her method starts in its development that fine type of independence of thought and action which comes only with mastery over one's self and one's environment.

In sharp contrast with the custom which makes the teacher the dominating figure in the schoolroom is the Montessori plan, which places her in the background lest the obtrusion of her influence should come to dominate the child. This respect for a child's personality has been many times expressed in one form or another, and thinkers from the time of Socrates have urged its importance. Indeed, it is merely the application of the law of all growth applied in the field of education. We keep our hands off the young bird or the young flower if we wish it to reach its fullest maturity. We must keep our hands off the child if we wish it to come to its highest self-realization. This principle of the necessity for allowing the peculiarities of the individuality to determine the direction of development is frequently ignored in our ordinary schools. Our universal error is to shape the child, somewhat unconsciously, but nevertheless definitely, according to our own prejudices. Such coercion is fatal to the advance of the race in a differentiated and ever ascending civilization.

Wherever there is organic life, circumstances must be favorable to the development of that particular organism, or it perishes. That the ancients observed this law is shown by the saying of Plutarch: "The soul is not a vase to be filled, but rather a hearth which is to be made to glow." And Rousseau says, speaking of Emile : "Now is the time for study. . . . It is not I who make the choice. It is pointed out to us by nature herself." The phrase of Comenius : "In all operations of nature, development is from within," shows that he also felt the force of this truth. In Pestalozzi's school there were no books, there were only natural objects, showing that he believed that the soul must be developed through what is within. Herbart, too, insists that "The teacher ought to make it a point of honor to leave the individuality as untouched as possible ; to leave it the only glory of which it is capable, namely, to be sharply definable even to conspicuousness."

Then Froebel, with remarkable vision, gathered up the theories of his predecessors, and, adding his own original insight, crystallized all that had been thus far apprehended into that wonderful scheme for development through self-activity — the kindergarten — exclaiming, "We must launch the child from birth into the free and all-sided use of its powers."

During the past twenty-five years, America has led the world in the child study movement. Much of this work centers about the belief that only free children can be profitably observed or make a normal development, and that the school of the future must deal with the individual child. President Jordan says, "The growth of individualism in education is the most promising feature in the social outlook of America." President Hall asserts, "The only safety lies in the study of and better adaptation to the nature and needs of childhood."

Especially strong is the statement of John Dewey, "Only by being true to the full growth of all the individuals who make it up, can society by any chance be true to itself." And in the same vein, President Harper says, "Individualism, coördination and association are the keynotes to future progress along educational lines."

Such are some of the mileposts which mark the progress of the ideal of freedom in the minds of educational reformers.

Now another one is added, and Doctor Montessori comes to us with the assertion that "All human virtues, all human progress, stand upon the inner force," that "No one can be free unless he is independent." She gives a radical illustration in her school of how these principles work out with young human beings. She has swept Italian teachers into the background, she has lifted the screws from seats in Italian schoolrooms, she has spread the walls to larger spaces. She has placed in children's hands self-corrective apparatus upon which they may exercise their powers. Best of all, she has freed the child's spirit, permitting him to think for himself, to use his own judgment and thus develop his own personality.

Thoughtful students who go into the Montessori schools recognize the operation of this principle. In referring to these schools, one does not mean the burlesques upon the idea which one may see in Rome, but the real Montessori schools where the method is applied with painstaking care. Ideal conditions are difficult of attainment at all times, but it gladdens one's eyes to

D

AFTER LUNCHEON THE DISHES MUST BE WASHED AND DRIED.

behold the theory of growth through self-activity being steadily applied and children happily responding to it. It is also a sight in sharp contrast to what one sees in other elementary schools in Rome and throughout Italy, and, therefore, the more striking. Indeed, in many places on the continent the teacher seems to be the dominating figure in the schoolroom and her word the children's law. The contrast between these schools, founded upon the military idea of discipline and domination, and Doctor Montessori's wise emphasis upon self-development through freedom and personal initiative is so great that the observer may be excused for using superlatives in describing what is seen. Even in Germany, where the kindergarten is native, there are many schools masquerading under that name which show scarcely any of the Froebelian spirit of freedom.

The writer once visited a Board school in London where there was that painful quiet of suppressed, inactive children. Only one boy out of fifty moved in his place, and when he swung his feet into the aisle to make the spine-curving seat less uncomfortable, he was sharply reproved, and the teacher said by the way of apology, "I have had this boy but two days." One knew this without being told, and sadly felt that the child would soon succumb to the wet blanket treatment and be as unnatural and "good" as the others. In her strong chapter on "Discipline," Doctor Montessori says:

"How shall one obtain discipline in a class of free children? Certainly in our system, we have a concept of discipline very different from that commonly accepted. If discipline is founded upon liberty, the discipline itself must necessarily be active. We do not consider an individual disciplined only when he has been rendered as artificially silent as a mute and as immovable as a paralytic. He is an individual annihilated, not disciplined.

"We call an individual disciplined when he is master of himself, and can, therefore, regulate his own conduct when it shall be necessary to follow some rule of life. Such a concept of active discipline is not easy either to comprehend or to apply. But certainly it contains a great educational principle, very different from the old time absolute and undiscussed coercion to immobility." [1]

The "directress," as Doctor Montessori prefers to call the teacher in her school, is not the most conspicuous person and the only really active agency in the schoolroom. She follows the lead of the scientist and is an observer of phenomena, interfering as little as is consistent with the logic of her theory. Doctor Montessori's own illustration of the purpose of teacher makes this point clear. She reminds us that the ideal guide who shows to a tourist a thing of artistic value simply says enough to enable the sightseer to understand and appreciate the object observed, then withdraws himself, for the *object* and not the *guide* is the center of interest. So the teacher must give necessary information and direction, then leave the child to think things out for himself. The garrulous teacher is an abomination to Doctor Montessori. She believes that the child smothered with words comprehends little that is said to him.

That mothers as well as teachers ignore this fact is illustrated by the incident of the child whose mother invited the kindergartener for luncheon. After the guest had arrived, the mother called: "Come out of the

[1] The Montessori Method, p. 86.

bathroom, Marie, Miss Smith is here and wishes to see you. Come, turn off the water and come out of the bathroom. You're not minding mother and you're getting your clean apron wet. Turn off the water and come out of the bathroom." After Marie had played in the water as long as she chose she came leisurely out and said, "Mother, your voice sounds just like a little bell: it goes tinkle, tinkle all the time."

Doctor Montessori's ideal of the function of the teacher is simply the natural response to the familiar clamor of the child, "Let me do it myself," "I can do it alone," "I know how to do it," constantly forced upon mothers and teachers, and as persistently put aside by many of them as they blindly follow the traditional method of doing for the child rather than allowing him to do for himself. Doctor Montessori resents this tendency of grown-ups to come between children and the things they are doing, to dominate and weaken intellects and wills, making children limp imitators and copyists. Her directress, like Froebel's ideal kindergartener, must be "passive, following, only guarding and protecting, not proscriptive, categorical, or interfering."

"Froebel had such unbounded faith in the right tendency of humanity, and such abhorrence of the idea of the 'total depravity' of childhood, that he taught in all his works that the teacher's duty is to place the child in proper conditions, and supply it with material adapted to its stage of development. Having done these things, he should reverently 'stand from between the child and God' and watch it grow, using his developed wisdom to study each individual child and adapt special conditions to guard it from evil and stimulate its best and fullest growth." [1]

[1] Froebel's Education Laws, Hughes, p. 156, D. Appleton & Co.

THE SILVER IS SORTED INTO BOXES AS A FINAL STEP IN
CLEARING AWAY THE LUNCHEON.

Though Doctor Montessori's emphasis upon the law of liberty and the process of self-expression takes from the teacher certain prerogatives, the teacher is of no small importance. She is a vitalizing force, her work calling for a high type of intelligence.

While she must follow the lead of the scientist and be an observer of natural phenomena, she must do more than this. Her natural phenomenon is the human soul. She must watch the unfolding life, to discern which acts hinder and which aid its growth; judging, measuring, estimating, making note of disordered movements and those that express content of thought; learning how she may help, but always keeping in mind that *the activity must come from within the child.* Thus in a spirit of love, service and reverence she may help human souls in their struggles toward the achievement of the self.

"When the teacher shall have touched, in this way, soul for soul, each one of her pupils, awakening and inspiring the life within them as if she were an invisible spirit, she will then possess each soul, and a sign, a single word, from her shall suffice; for each one will feel her in a living and vital way, will recognize her and will listen to her. There will come a day when the directress herself shall be filled with wonder to see that all the children obey her with gentleness and affection, not only ready, but intent, at a sign from her." [1]

The patience exhibited by Doctor Montessori is no doubt the outgrowth of long, untiring efforts to awaken the groping faculties of feeble-minded children, with whom hurry or confusion would produce utter failure. Normal children can and do endure much nagging at

[1] The Montessori Method, p. 116.

the hands of adults, but it has its evil effect in sapping their nervous energy and vitality.

Dorothy Canfield Fisher, in describing her first visit to a Montessori school, says :

"That collection of little tots, most of them too busy over their mysterious occupations even to talk, seemed, as far as a casual glance over the room went, entirely without supervision. Finally, from a corner, where she had been sitting (on the floor apparently) beside a child, there rose up a plainly dressed woman, the expression of whose quiet face made almost as great an impression on me as the children's greetings had. . . . She lingered beside us some moments. I noticed that she happened to stand all the time with her back to the children, feeling apparently none of that lion-tamer's instinct to keep an hypnotic eye on the little animals which is so marked in our instructors. I can remember distinctly that there was for us school children actually a different feel to the air and a strange look on the familiar school furniture during those infrequent intervals when the teacher was called for an instant from the room and left us, as in a suddenly rarefied atmosphere, giddy with the removal of the pressure of her eye. But when this teacher turned about casually to face the room again, these children did not seem to notice either that she had stopped looking at them or that she was now doing it again.

"We used to know, as by a sixth sense, exactly where, at any moment, the teacher was, and a sudden movement on her part would have made us all start as violently and as instinctively as little chicks at the sudden shadow of a hawk . . . and this, although we were often very fond indeed of our teachers. Remembering this, I noticed with surprise that often when one of these little ones lifted his face from his work to ask the teacher a question, he had been so unconscious of her presence during his concentration on his enterprise that he did not know in the least where to look, and sent his eager eyes roving over the big room in a search for her." [1]

[1] A Montessori Mother, Dorothy Canfield Fisher, pp. 10-12, Henry Holt & Co.

The temptation is to do for children the things they might do for themselves, ignoring the great law of growth, which is that strength comes only through struggle, and that effort often gives greater pleasure than result. The overcoming of obstacles, the mastering of difficulties, gives more real joy than the achievement when it is reached.

It calls for much greater intelligence, tact and skill, to direct thirty active, energetic little beings, all free to move and choose for themselves, than to control that many seated in rows, who are not allowed to speak or even turn in their seats without permission. Teachers are often pronounced a success because they keep good order, when, in reality, this discipline by force need not presuppose one desirable quality in the teacher. The great test comes when children are given their freedom. If they behave in an unnatural way, and do not know how to use it, if they show lack of self-control and judgment, turning freedom into license, their actions tell of suppression and restraint. But if, on the contrary, children are self-directive and coöperative among their fellows, we know that they are gradually being liberated from the necessity of outward control. Doctor Montessori uses the word " discipline" in referring to training rather than controlling. She encourages in children a kind of independence which comes only with the consciousness of personal power and deep-seated self-respect.

"Growth and independence involve that true discipline which comes through work. For as Montessori well says, 'Discipline is a path, not a fact, it is a means, not an end,' and the very beginning of it appears when the child, keenly interested in doing,

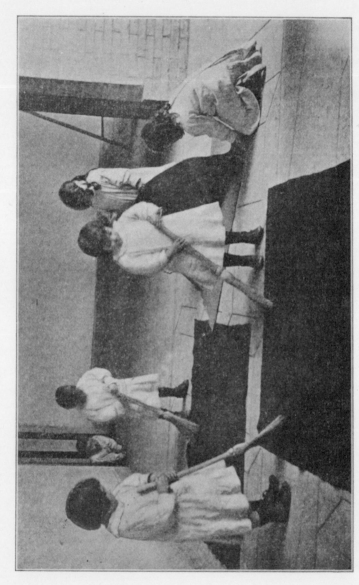

ANOTHER HOUSEHOLD ACTIVITY. RUGS MUST BE SWEPT AND FOLDED BEFORE BEING PUT AWAY.

sets himself to the accomplishment of a definite task. It is attained indirectly through the direction of a child's own spontaneous efforts. It needs for its perfection the repetition of a series of complete acts through work which he instinctively desires and toward which he naturally turns and by means of which, as he gains more and more power and freedom, he sets his personality in order and sees new possibilities of growth." [1]

There is a natural sequence in the developing process as it applies to obedience. There is first the unconscious, unawakened spiritual disorder of the unmoral being. Then the awakened consciousness, the separation from the self, the struggle toward obedience, and later the power to do through a deepened consciousness, the development of will, intelligence and social spirit; the adjusting of the inner self to the outside world; joyous obedience, spiritual order, freedom.

Doctor Theodate Smith has expressed Doctor Montessori's concept in the following way:

"When in the first, confused stage the child does not obey a command, it is as if he were psychically deaf. He hears, but does not understand. In the second stage he seems to understand, but has not yet the complete command of his inner process that enables him to complete the external act promptly, and we say that he is not quick to mind. In the third stage he obeys promptly and cheerfully, showing pride in his knowledge of how to obey. A child thus trained is not only obedient, but he is self-disciplined and has acquired a poise and calm that orders his actions and deepens and enlarges his moral life. This analysis of Dr. Montessori's is entirely in accord with the results of special studies of obstinacy which show this to be not, as is popularly supposed, evidence of a strong will, but as due rather to a weakness of will, which the

[1] A Guide to the Montessori Method, Ellen Yale Stevens, p. 33. Frederick A. Stokes Company.

child cannot overcome. He may even wish to obey, and yet persist in his disobedience from inability to overcome the psychic cramp. Some of these cases are real tragedies of childhood which might be avoided by an enlightened teaching of obedience." [1]

If one follows the Montessori line of thinking, it is easy to understand why she taboos all manner of the more material and physical prizes and punishments, believing that success or achievement on the part of the child is in itself sufficient reward, that failure is merely an indication that the child has not reached that point in his development where he is ready for the thing attempted. If a child is skillful with his hands, it is because he has gained that kind of motor control, coupled with intellect and will power, which makes such skill possible and enjoyable to him. The thing accomplished, being the result of his development, calls for no more special credit or praise than the act of running or jumping in play. Even the effort which the result cost came in response to an inner impulse which it would have been difficult for the child to resist.

Have you not seen the look of surprise on the face of a child when praised for a thing he had done with great pleasure and without conscious effort? Perhaps you have seen this same child come to overestimate his effort because of unnatural stimulus and settle back to indifference.

Failure in a bit of handiwork should cause us to make the opposite inference. The child is not up to this particular activity as yet. To attach undue importance to his failure, to blame, punish or humiliate him is to

[1] The Montessori System, Theodate L. Smith, p. 44. Harper and Brothers.

magnify his fault and thus to give him wrong notions about himself.[1]

If one stops to think of it, the excessive use of praise and blame, prize and punishment, is indulged in primarily by the mothers and teachers whose ideals are not the highest. The teacher who wishes to force all children into a certain position of body or action of mind will invariably resort to these incentives. The mother who desires to dispose of all questions with the least possible thought or trouble to herself will use these means, often showing great annoyance and punishing severely for a slight fault, and praising profusely or rewarding extravagantly a slight exhibition of virtue.

A certain father and mother were called next door to see the grandmother, who was ill, and in the emergency they left two small sisters to care for themselves. On their return at bedtime both children were asleep. To their gratification they found that the older sister had covered the little one with the only available blanket. When the children awoke the father impulsively said: "You were a very good girl to take such care of little sister. Here is twenty-five cents to pay you for it."

The next night there was a repetition of the occurrence. Father and mother were again called out. This time older sister forcibly compelled little sister to lie down and be covered up, though she was neither sleepy nor cold. The first night the child had acted on a generous, kindly impulse which needed no reward. On the second occasion her motive had dropped to a lower level.

Doctor Montessori urges us not to judge children by

[1] The Child, Tanner, Chapter X.

the standards of adults. Their love of activity, their
curiosity, their impulsiveness, sometimes lead them into
wrong acts whose motives are innocent of wrong. Therefore, we should try to judge by motives rather than conduct, gradually pointing out the relation of cause and

THE BUTTONING AND LACING FRAMES.

effect, and training the intelligence and will to voluntary obedience. In the Montessori school, the positive
side of the child's nature is built up and little faults are
often apparently ignored, though the scientific directress
makes mental note of them with a view of strengthening
any apparent weakness.

Doctor Montessori believes that in this particular
period of the child's growth, a certain amount of selfish-

ness is not only natural but necessary. If the child is forced into social obligations beyond his years, his future is made ineffective. Professor Kirkpatrick tells us that the selfishness of a young child is necessary to his development. "If the will is weakened, the individual is weakened, and is of no force in society."

When the child first comes into contact with a group of his own age he is quite unwilling to share. He reaches out as far as he can and draws all the blocks to himself. A little egotist, he must grow into altruism by experience with the social group.

When we expect that the child will always "go back of the lady instead of in front of her"; that she will always express appreciation for every service, we are forgetting that the forms that seem easy for us because of long years of contact with people are neither natural nor necessary for the child. One mother said to her child: "Did you thank the lady for the apple?" "Oh, yes, mother," said the child, "I thanked her but I didn't tell her so."

Montessori would place within the reach of children that sort of an environment which will make it possible for them to carry on a sort of process of self-making. With every physical comfort provided, with didactic material which provokes investigation and experiment within prescribed limits, with plants and pets to be nourished and cared for, she would establish among the children a kind of miniature community where each child looking into eyes on a level with his own may test his strength and skill with others of his own stature, may practice promptness, courtesy, consideration for others,

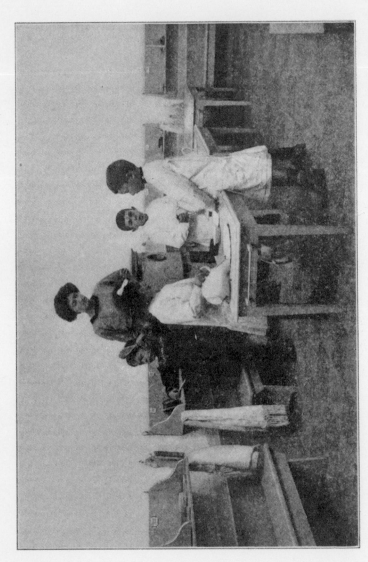

LITTLE ARISTOCRATS LEARNING TO BRUSH THEIR HAIR, WASH THEIR HANDS AND CARRY PITCHERS OF WATER WITHOUT THE HELP OF A MAID. — PINCIAN HILL SCHOOL.

"He who is served is limited in his independence." — MONTESSORI.

neatness, order and accuracy, while gaining some notions of the fundamentals of the social virtues by dealing with real social problems.

Every striking feature of Doctor Montessori's school may be traced directly to the reverence she feels for that divine spark of selfhood in the child which makes it possible for each individual to make his own contribution to society. Every violation of formal school régime, from the radical forms of liberty to the auto-educational materials, has as an aim the freeing of the child through self-activity.[1]

One who would judge this method fairly must keep constantly in mind this purpose of its originator and hold himself open-minded toward its exemplification. It is easy for the timid to hold any theory as an impracticable ideal.   It is an epoch-making event when a high-spirited student and champion of childhood makes the venture of faith and gives full trial to the theory in its working day by day in a schoolroom.

The technique, the method of securing this liberty, may be critically considered and weighed, but as to the fundamental idea, no intelligent twentieth century educator will quarrel with Doctor Montessori in her emphasis upon the inalienable right of every child to free, natural, unhampered growth.   In her strong plea for liberty found in the fifth chapter of her book, she says:

"We cannot know the consequences of suffocating a spontaneous action at the time when the child is just beginning to be active: perhaps we suffocate life itself.   Humanity shows itself in all its intellectual splendor during this tender age as the sun

[1] The Individual in the Making, Kirkpatrick, Chapter VI.

shows itself at the dawn, and the flower in the first unfolding of the petals; and we must respect religiously, reverently, these first indications of individuality. If any educational act is to be efficacious, it will be that alone which tends to help toward the complete unfolding of this life." [1]

The fact that this principle of liberty is not new to educators should not detract from the honor we give this wise Italian woman, for though we have recognized the theory, do the rank and file of us live up to it in our pedagogic practice? Are we not in our daily contact with children inclined to suppress, subdue, control, to make a fetish of order, to demand grown-up standards, to require children to think our thoughts after us? Do we not take words out of their mouths and work out of their hands? Do we not lead rather than follow in many of their activities? So long as these things are true (and who will deny them) and until we have brought this ideal of freedom out of the realm of theory and put it into general practice, we who are teachers should welcome each new illustration of this fundamental principle.

Though some may not agree with certain of Doctor Montessori's more radical ideas, the widespread interest and discussion of this method is prophetic of a better day for all children, and since the children of that day will constitute the social group when they are mature, it is prophetic, too, of a higher plane of citizenship.

[1] The Montessori Method, p. 87.

POINTS FOR DISCUSSION

1. Name some common practices in our elementary schools that violate the principle of freedom as formulated by Montessori.

2. Illustrate and explain the statement that only free children can be profitably observed.

3. Why is it so easy for the teacher or parent to form the habit of dominating the child? Give the effects of such domination (a) upon the child, (b) upon the adult.

4. Show that the principle of freedom does not conflict with training children for social coöperation.

5. In applying this principle of freedom in the home and the school, what mistakes are parents and teachers very apt to make?

6. Why are the teachings of our greatest educational writers so persistently ignored in our educational practice?

7. Describe a schoolroom that in your judgment would best conform to the principle of freedom.

8. Compare the evils of repressing the child's activities with the evils of the incorrect expression of his activities.

9. Give illustrations of the effects upon the child, (a) of overpraise, (b) of too harsh censure.

10. Compare Doctor Montessori's methods and ideals with Pestalozzi's as formulated in "How Gertrude Teaches Her Children."

CHAPTER IV

THE CHILD'S WORLD OF OBJECTS

THE world is without form and void to the tiny infant, when "Mother's eyes are baby's skies" and when the limp fingers vaguely clutch at the soft blanket. At first, tastes and odors, sights and sounds, are not heeded. What comes to be ordered consciousness is in earliest infancy only capacity or unawakened potentialities.

This capacity resides in a physical mechanism appearing to have a "perpetual motion" endowment. To the uninitiated, all the throwing about of arms and legs, the opening and shutting of hands and eyes seems like a waste of energy. It has taken mankind some hundreds of thousands of years to appreciate the real significance of these first movements. Only recently has the very long "first dress" given way to a shorter one which encourages the abundance of physical activity ordained by Nature for the child's growth. The swaddling clothes of the "Bambino," the cradle of the papoose, are painful reminders of the older order of things.

Movements bring the child into contact with his strange new world, but the experience of a movement resulting in a particular contact means so little in the beginning that it is difficult to describe. It is little more than "awareness" due to a change from the state of non-movement and general contact to one of movement and particular contact. Some later recurrence of this particular experience will have a tinge of familiarity, a feeling element in this state of "awareness." This feeling of "having met before" is the germ of memory. When, at the presentation of one of the regularly involved stimuli to the appropriate sense organ, the remembrance or image is sufficiently vivid to control the repetition of the whole activity, "the beginning of the organized consciousness" may be said to be present. It would no doubt surprise many parents to realize that the child's mind cannot organize itself without countless and varied movements. The purpose of 'movement is popularly supposed to be the acquiring of control of the body in holding up the head, sitting, standing, and doing things with the hands, whereas the purpose of the sense organs is supposed to be the awakening and developing of the mind.

There are two groups of defective conditions found in children. In the first group the physical equipment for tactile-motor activity is normal, but that of the sense organs of sight, hearing, taste, and smell is wholly or partially lacking. In the second group the sense organs are normal but the power of moving the trunk, head, and limbs is reduced very close to the level of paralysis.

Which one of these two groups of defective conditions is more serious in a young child, judged from the standpoint of his capacity to develop into a human being, is clear when we compare the case of Helen Keller with that of a defective child of the opposite type.

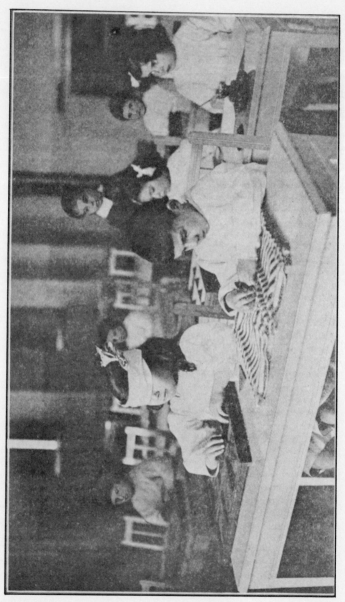

The "Seeing" Fingers.

Helen Keller's handicaps did not extend to the taste and smell senses; she gives them much credit for making experiences varied and rich. Gesell says, "Read her fine encomiums of the 'black sheep' senses, taste and smell, and you will realize that the very foundation of her spiritual power is rooted in the wealth of emotion derived from the loving use of these bodily senses." Her most direct avenue of approach to intelligence, however, has been through "motor-tactile communion" with her environment.

The case representing the other group of defective conditions is familiar to any one who has seen the vegetative existence of the child in whose nervous system the motor or the associative neurons, or both, do not perform their work except in the elementary physiological functions of respiration, circulation, digestion and excretion. "Human life" is not possible for such a child, though the sense organs are not structurally imperfect. Their development is of course arrested, because of the absence of the contacts which muscular and tactile activity would have brought.

To one who has read Doctor Montessori's book, it is evident that she places a high value upon motor-sensory development. She believes (1) that the home and the school have not realized its importance and inter-relations, (2) that they have identified immobility with order and goodness, and mobility with disorder and naughtiness, (3) that they have overvalued sight and hearing, and undervalued (to the verge of ignoring them) the tactile-muscular activities, and (4) that they have too seldom sought to know and to correct curable defects and to plan systematic training exercises with suitable materials.

Referring to this, G. Stanley Hall says,

" For many years, sense training has been theoretically commended and practically discouraged. Educators lay themselves open to a peculiar charge who insist that all knowledge has its foundation in the senses, and who yet see that almost all a child's time allotted to study is taken up with poring over books."

Experts in any line, and artists, with power to see, hear, and appreciate much that is lost to the average man, illustrate what the senses may become through exercise. Such exercise should not be overdone nor placed out of its natural relationships, but childhood is a time of great importance for the storing up of satisfying experiences with *things*, and if this period is allowed to slip by without such experiences, later life is impoverished.[1] If parents and teachers realized this close relation between sensori-motor activities and growth, the average home and school environment would be enriched by much that is now lacking, and greater freedom would be granted the child. There would be also careful observations which would result in tests to ascertain the exact physical condition of the sense organs. Sometimes after years of blundering, a teacher or parent discovers that a supposedly dull or apparently degenerate child has some slight obstruction to the natural sensory activity which causes a derangement of behavior.[2]

[1] Principles of Educational Practice, Klapper, Chapters V, VI.
[2] The Story of the Mind, Baldwin, Chapter V. Provision for Exceptional Children in Public Schools, U. S. Bureau of Education, Bulletin 1911, No. 14.

It seems a far call from the child's disordered chaos of sense impressions to the man's ordered cosmos of inner consciousness, but the definite and close connection between early sense impressions and later bodily health, mental alertness, and spiritual insight is close and exact. Hence the child's future happiness, intelligence and efficiency depend in a large measure upon three conditions.

First. Healthy normal sense organs capable of receiving stimuli from the outer world.

Second. The power of the mind to take up, assimilate and use these materials of sense impressions, transforming them into creative ideas with a dynamic tendency — that is, a tendency to go out in some form of expression.

Third. A developing nervous system consisting of (1) sensory nerves; (2) sensory areas of the cortex; (3) motor areas of the cortex; (4) connective or associative fibers joining these two areas of the cortex; (5) motor nerves terminating in the muscles. This is the mechanism that enables the child to acquire the mastery of his environment.

Equal in importance to this perfectly working sensorimotor apparatus, is an environment which is rich in opportunity for its stimulation. No child can grow normally in surroundings which are barren of natural interests, which provide only for grown-up tastes, and where everything is just out of reach of tingling fingers or not suitable for the use of small investigators.

In considering a child's environment, one should keep in mind that his prime interest in the objects that surround him is in what he can do with them. In other words, their different qualities seem to come to consciousness as demanded for appropriate behavior.[1] The simple toys given to the baby are chosen upon the basis of the way they respond to his various activities. The rattle that goes into his hand and his mouth, its various sounds as he shakes it or strikes it against another object, makes it appeal through the ear. The ball that can be subjected to the hand and mouth activities, its movement as it rolls away or falls, catches the eye. It calls for reaching (or for waiting for others to do so) and returning. The blocks that can be put in and taken out of their box countless times, that can later be piled up and tumbled over, are typical examples of playthings which satisfy the instinctive tendency to be active and which lead to simple motor coördinations and elemental sensory impressions; for consciousness develops according to the demands made upon it for adjustment. As time goes on, other toys are given to the child — toys which are imitations of processes and objects in the world of man and nature. Sounds, colors, movements, textures, densities, weights and temperatures are revealing themselves not only through these playthings, but also through the actual life of adults.

So we see that early impressions of objects are so wrapped up in motor activity that it is difficult to analyze them or to tell when they are acquired. King says, "It is possible that the emphasis remains very largely on the activity rather than the thing until the child is five or six years of age. Later, things, as such,

[1] The Psychology of Child Development, King, Chapter V. The University of Chicago.

stand out; and still later, the complex system of ends which they may serve come to be interesting."

With the introduction of such materials as sand, blocks, clay, colored crayons, paints, scissors, and paper, the world of sensori-motor activity is tremendously extended, for the time comes when the doing of an act reaches the level of control by definite and related ideas. Making miniature objects or pictures of objects is a more highly organized reaction upon environment than the early instinctive handling, tasting, and pounding responses to stimuli.

In addition to an environment containing (1) abundant sensory stimuli, adapted to the child's particular stage of growth, and (2) opportunity for varied ways of expressing the impressions received by reaction upon environment, there should be (3) frequent repetition of impression, reaction and expression.

"Don't touch," is an easy thing to say and is often a protection to bric-a-brac or china, but one might as well say to a child, "Don't grow," "Don't learn," "Don't try to understand." He takes to touching as he takes to eating, and it is fortunate that he does so, for the mind cannot get on without sense food any more than the body can grow without nourishment. The small fingers clasp about the apple. The short arms try to encircle a tree trunk. The cushioned finger tips stroke pussy's fur. Every surface, every solid, every liquid within tiptoe-reach is challenged to tell of its texture, its size, its dimensions, its weight, its temperature, by the way it responds to the subtlest of sense organs — touch.

THE SENSE OF TOUCH.

The use of **textures** refines tactile discrimination.

Sometimes touch is defective; more often it is un-developed. To understand what it may contribute to life, one must turn to such cases as those already referred to. One blind student when asked if he would have his sight restored replied: "If it were not for curiosity, I would rather have long arms. It seems to me that my hands would teach me better what is pass-ing in the moon than your eyes or telescope." Helen Keller's marvelous power to "see" through delicate finger tips is illustrated by her visit to an art gallery, where she enjoyed many statues with her seeing fingers. Moving them lightly over the marble "Melancholy," she remarked, "This face feels sad." Many a woman of normal vision had passed that statue without catching the sculptor's motive, but Helen Keller, through the mastery of form gained by the use of touch, the funda-mental sense, has acquired a culture possessed by few other women of our time. So we see that this so-called "lower" sense may be of the highest value and sig-nificance, not only for intellectual perception but for soul awakening as well.

Helen Keller says:

"I only know that the world I see with my fingers is alive, ruddy, and satisfying. Touch brings the blind many sweet cer tainties which our more fortunate fellows miss because their sense of touch is uncultivated. In touch is all love and intelligence.

"The thousand soft voices of the earth have truly found their way to me — the small rustle in tufts of grass, the silky swish of leaves, the buzz of insects, the hum of bees in blossoms I have plucked, the flutter of a bird's wings after his bath, and the slender rippling vibration of water running over pebbles. Once having been felt, these loved voices rustle, buzz, hum, flutter, and ripple in my thought forever, an undying part of happy memories."

"In the realms of wonderment where I dwell
I explore life with my hands;
I recognize, and am happy;
My fingers are ever athirst for the earth,
And drink up its wonders with delight,
Draw out earth's dear delights;
My feet are charged with the murmur,
The throb, of all things that grow.

"This is touch, this quivering,
This flame, this ether,
This glad rush of blood,
This daylight in my heart,
This glow of sympathy in my palms.
Thou blind, loving, all-prying touch,
Thou openst the book of life to me.
The noiseless little noises of earth
Come with softest rustle;
The shy, sweet feet of life;
The silky flutter of moth wings
Against my restraining palm." [1]

Passages from Helen Keller are quoted in the chapter on "Touch" in that fascinating book "The Normal Child and Primary Education." The authors say of her:

"Well may she sing a Chant of Darkness, for in this darkness touch is quickened, and in touch lives the deepest appreciation of things.

"Though we cannot develop in every child the wonderful sensibility of Helen Keller, we can have more respect for the deep values that lie hidden in touch. They are often vague, and nearly always inarticulate. Because these values cannot be put into words they have no recognition in the schools; but they can be communicated by teachers who show an enthusiasm for simple things."

[1] The World I Live In, Helen Keller, pp. 42, 59, 191. The Century Co.

On another page they say:

"A little child may stroke a soft blanket with a delight so intense, and yet so reverent and tender, as to be almost spiritual. Through no other avenue does the child get such a wealth of artistic enjoyment. Who can number the thrills of pleasure every eager child gains by the mere stroking of smooth surfaces and rondures, polished woods and marbles, pebbles, silks, vegetables, fruits, animals? And what of the endless rapturous experiments with the textures, the pliancy, elasticity, and rigidity of all sorts of materials?

" Then there are the larger dermal joys and adventures in which face and cheek, and sometimes the whole body, participate, — the big tactual experiences with the elements, fire, frost, cold, wind, mist, sod, beach, and sea. These massy experiences, though less descriminative than the delicate touches of the finger tips, are all the more bucolic and exuberant, for they are profoundly dyed with the interests, joys, and longings of the race; and there is a resurgence of feeling when the child reëxperiences them. Hence his orgy of enjoyment when he is free to wade, wallow, and splash in mud or water. Bareheadedness, barefootedness — and on swimming and athletic days, barebodiedness — are the biological rights of every child. Only by such generous exposure to wind and weather, to earth, water, and sky, can nature make those rich, massive impressions which get to the depth of the soul. Every child needs a rich range of touch experiences, — of the delicate for the appreciation of things refined, of the grosser for the appreciation of things strong, stately, and sublime."[1]

Later in life, sight takes from touch much of its responsibility, but the accuracy of eyesight depends in large measure upon the touch and motor experiences of childhood in regard to form, texture, direction and distance. We grow to depend upon touch less as the

[1] The Normal Child and Primary Education, by Arnold L. and Beatrice C. Gesell, pp. 112–114. Ginn & Co.

eye through visual and muscular sensations symbolizes touch sensations, and gives us the information which touch at first supplied.

"The intellectual value of touch, the power to give us knowledge of the external world, is seldom placed high enough. Without the sense of touch the child would not only see things flat, but the myriad forms that fill the earth and sky would never be known to him. All of them would be alike to him — neither rough nor smooth, fine nor coarse, sharp nor blunt, round nor square, far nor near, in high nor low relief. In fact, he would have no idea in the concrete or in the abstract of any such qualities. He would in manhood be tumbling downstairs, over chairs, into the fireplace, into the washtub, and everywhere else, just as he does in childhood before this sense has taught him the relief and relations of objects. Without it he would know neither sea nor land, wood nor mineral. If man were deprived of the sense of touch, every loom, every ship, every railway car, every industry in which man is engaged, would instantly stop. All these are dependent upon its high cultivation for their successful conduct." [1]

While special emphasis should be placed upon touch, provision should also be made for enriching the sensory life of the child through sight, hearing, taste and smell.

Sight may bring to the child a world of beauty in tints and tone, light and shade, and graceful arrangement. He may acquire the spiritual possession of everything within the range of his horizon by the medium of this æsthetic sense, or he may become aware only of the commonplace. To look without observing is the habit of those who "having eyes to see, see not."

Hearing, too, is so closely associated with the best and most refining influences of life that the importance of

[1] The Study of the Child, Taylor, p. 29. D. Appleton & Co.

caring for its organ and training its powers of discrimination can scarcely be overestimated. To catch the
varied music of the out-of-doors, the song of water, tree
or bird, the subtle lights and shades of speech, the rich
tones of an organ, is to have the emotional nature stirred,
and to be lifted to higher levels of thought.

Taste and smell — two outposts of the body — stand
ready to protect and guard the child's physical comfort
and lead him to finer discriminations in matters of
ethical taste.

Perhaps no one has better expressed the true significance of sense organs and their activity than has Froebel,
who says :

"Every external object comes to man with the invitation to
determine its nature and relationships. For this he has senses,
the organs that enable him to meet that invitation.

"The early beginnings of education are most important because
they give a bias to all after-development. Early education must
deal with the physical development and influence the spiritual
development through the exercise of the senses." [1]

His Mother Play motto on The Revelation of Sense
runs thus :

"As each new life is given to the world,
The senses — like a door that swings two ways —
Stand ever 'twixt its inner, waiting self
And that environment with which its lot
Awhile is cast.

"A door that swings two ways:
Inward at first it turns, while Nature speaks,
To greet her guest and bid him to her feast,

[1] Education of Man, Froebel, Chapter II. D. Appleton & Co.

F

And tell him of all things in her domain,
The good or ill of each, and how to use;
Then outward, to set free an answering thought.
And so, swift messages fly back and forth
Without surcease — until, behold! she, who
Like gracious host received a timid guest,
Owns in that guest at length her rightful lord,
And gladly serves him, asking no reward!
This parable, dear mother, is for you,
Whom God has made his steward for your child.
All Nature is a unit in herself,
Yet but a part of a far greater whole.
Little by little you may teach your child
To know her ways, and live in harmony
With her; and then, in turn, help him through her
To find those verities within himself,
Of which all outward things are but the type." [1]

The broad sweep of this motto suggests the carrying over of the basic conception of physical taste into a higher field where conduct is estimated by a sweet spirit, a soft answer or a well-rounded day. As impressions enter the "door that swings two ways" the child begins a lifelong process of arranging, organizing and modifying his environment. Not satisfied with its appearance, he learns its essence as well. Discrimination and choice begin to appear; judgment and will are developed; and, as he makes over his environment to meet his needs, he makes himself over in the process, struggling ever toward that highest goal of mankind, which is self-realization through self-activity. When we consider how much surroundings have to do with the attainment of this goal,

[1] Mottoes and Commentaries of Froebel's Mother Play, Blow. D. Appleton & Co.

we find ourselves asking, what shall the child's eyes rest upon? What shall his fingers touch, his ears hear, his palate taste, his nostrils inhale? Walt Whitman's poem is suggestive here.

"There was a child went forth every day,
  And the first object he looked upon, that object he became,
  And that object became part of him for the day or a certain part
      of the day,
  Or for many years or stretching cycles of years.

" The early lilacs became part of this child,
  And grass and white and red morning-glories, and white and
      red clover, and the song of the phœbe bird,
  And the third-month lambs and the sow's pink-faint litter, and
      the mare's foal and the cow's calf,
  And the noisy brood of the barnyard or by mire of the pond side,
  And the fish suspending themselves so curiously below there,
      and the beautiful curious liquid,
  And the water plants with their graceful flat heads, all be-
      came part of him." [1]

The nature and value of healthy, vigorous, sensory activity and its relation to mental and moral awakening is recognized by all students of child psychology, but no other educator has offered for normal children a plan so elaborate and exact for sense gymnastics, nor gained by a sequence of developing exercises such marked results as has Doctor Montessori. Regarding her didactic materials, she makes the following points clear in " The Montessori Method."

First. Many of these materials were not invented by her, although modified and perfected to meet the needs of normal children.

[1] Leaves of Grass, Whitman.   David McKay, Publisher.

Second. Some of the materials are similar to those used in experimental psychology, but the process does not grow out of the conclusions of experimental psychology. The one is a testing process often consuming the energy of the child, the other is an educative process developing the energies of the child.

Third. While the materials make education possible for defectives, they provoke auto-education with normal children.

Fourth. Because the materials are self-corrective, they minimize the teacher's activity.

Fifth. Materials are presented by the lesson plan of Seguin which contains three steps :

a. The association of sensory perception with name.

b. The recognition of objects by name.

c. The remembering of the name which corresponds to the object.

Sixth. The procedure is from a few sharply contrasted stimuli to many stimuli with slighter shades of difference.

Seventh. Errors are not corrected ; materials are put aside until another time on the supposition that the child who fails to grasp the point of the lesson is not ready for it.

Eighth. Much instruction is individual, but the children often form themselves into groups.

Ninth. Efforts are sometimes made to isolate the sense activities in order to intensify the functioning of a given one.

Tenth. The interference of the teacher is to be reduced to a minimum so as not to deprive the child of his right to cope with his own problems.

Eleventh. All lessons are simple, concise and objective.

The materials designed for the education of the various senses are fully described and their use explained in "The Montessori Method," Chapters XII, XIII. They are here briefly grouped, as obtainable in America.[1]

I. Touch.

Material.

    a. A rectangular board divided into two equal parts, one having the surface smoothly polished, the other covered with sandpaper. (Fig. 1.)

FIG. 1.

    b. A board like the preceding, the surface of which is divided crosswise into alternate strips of board and sandpaper. (Fig. 1.)

    c. A collection of paper strips varying from fine cardboard to coarse sandpaper.

    d. A chest of drawers containing pieces of typical kinds of cloth, velvet, wool, crash, silk, cotton and linen. (Fig. 2.)

" From an evolution point of view touch is the first distinctly differentiated sensation, and this primary position it still holds in our mental life." — JAMES' *Psychology.* Henry Holt & Co.

[1] The House of Childhood, 200 Fifth Ave., New York manufacturers.

" If the child's knowledge reaches to a solid foundation of sense training, the floods of time will beat in vain upon that knowledge. Other things may pass away, but that remains while the brain lasts." — HALLECK.[1]

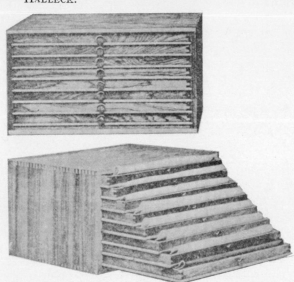

FIG. 2.

"They do verily exercise the tactile sense. They enjoy keenly touching any soft pleasant surface and become exceedingly keen in discriminating between the differences in the sandpaper cards." — MONTESSORI.

II. Temperature.

> Material. — Metal bowls filled with water of varying degrees of temperature, with thermometer for testing.

"It would appear that certain nerve filaments have special temperature functions entirely distinct from those of touch." — TAYLOR.

[1] Education of Central Nervous System, Halleck. The Macmillan Co.

"I also have the children put their hands into cold, tepid and warm water, an exercise which they find most diverting." — MONTESSORI.

III. Weight.
    Material. — Small wooden tablets, of pine, walnut and wistaria weighing respectively 24, 18 and 12 grams. (Fig. 3.)

FIG. 3.

"The game attracts the attention of those near, who gather in a circle about the one who has the tablets and who take turns in guessing. Sometimes the children spontaneously make use of the blindfold, taking turns and interspersing the work with peals of laughter." — MONTESSORI.

IV. Muscular and Tactile.
    Material.
        a. Twelve each of Froebel's third gift and fourth gift blocks.
        b. Miscellaneous objects.

" The most fundamental data for our perception of distance, direction, size, and form come through the feel gate. Only handling and manual activity can put vividness and content into the perceptions of the outside world. The child must begin in very infancy its acquaintance with the resistance and construction qualities of paper, sand, cloth and word." — GESELL.

V. Sight.

  Material.

  1. Dimensions.

    (1) Solid Insets. — This material consists of three series of wooden cylinders set in corresponding holes in solid blocks of wood 55 × 8 × 6 centimeters in dimension. Each series contains ten cylinders. In the first, the

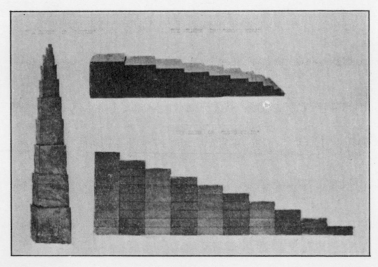

FIG. 4.

diameter varies; in the second, the height; and in the third, both the diameter and height.

    (2) The Tower. — A series of ten wooden cubes decreasing in size

one centimeter each from a base
of ten centimeters to a base of one
centimeter. (Fig. 4.)

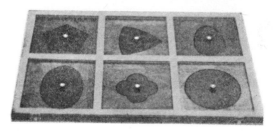

FIG. 5.

(3) The Broad Stair. — A set of ten
    wooden blocks decreasing in size
    from a base of ten centimeters
    as found in the largest to a base
    of one centimeter as found in
    the smallest. The length which

is constant is twenty centimeters.
(Fig. 4.)

(4) The Long Stair. — A set of ten
rods, the first being one meter in
length; the last, one decimeter;
the intervening rods diminishing
one decimeter each. The spaces
on each rod are painted alternately
red and blue. (Fig. 4.)

2. Form.   (For both sight and touch.)

a. Plane geometric insets of wood,
consisting of a six-drawer
cabinet containing (Fig. 5):

(1) Four plane wooden squares and
two frames contain a rhom-
boid and a trapezoid.

(2) Six polygons.

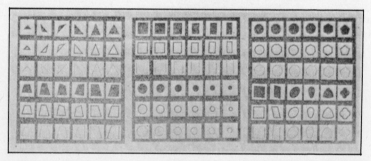

FIG. 6.

(3) Six circles diminishing in size.
(4) Six quadrilaterals containing
one square and five rectangles.
(5) Six triangles.
(6) A variety of forms.

b. Plane Geometric Forms. (Fig. 6.)

(1) Cards containing blue patterns the size of the insets found in *a*.

(2) Cards whereon the same figures are represented by outlines of blue paper. (Fig. 6.)

(3) Cards upon which are drawn in black the narrow outlines of the same figures. (Fig. 6.)

FIG. 7.

3. Color.

a. Two boxes of eight compartments each, containing 64 color tablets. These are of red, orange, yellow, green, blue, violet, black and brown, presented in a series

of eight tints and shades.
(Fig. 7.)

    b. Brightly colored stuffs and balls.

"Of all the silent teachers that influence us from our entrance into this world to our going out of it, color is perhaps the most subtle and most mysterious." — HARRISON.

"Proceed from a few stimuli strongly contrasting to many stimuli in gradual differentiation always more fine and imperceptible." — MONTESSORI.

VI. Hearing.

Material.

    a. Cylindrical boxes containing sand and pebbles which when shaken produce sound varying in volume and tone. (Fig. 8.)

FIG. 8.

    b. Bells varying in volume and pitch.
    c. Whistles varying in volume and pitch.
    d. Drums and bells (graded).
    e. Stringed instruments.
    f. Voice.
    g. Silence and whisper-tests of accurate hearing.

VII. Taste.

> Material. — Various solutions, acid, sweet, salt,
> bitter.

"Taste is an outpost of the whole system for enabling it to assimilate the beneficial and reject the harmful." — DEWEY.

VIII. Smell.

> Material. — Flower and food odors.

> "All these pretty flowers
> Have their own sweet smell,
> Often without seeing
> We their names can tell.

> "So our eyes we cover
> That we may not see
> While the fragrance tells us
> What the flower must be." [1] — POULSSON.

"The best way to look at nature is to recognize it as a body of educative materials pressing upon the children from all sides and calling out their activities and impressively iterating the simplest real lessons." — McMURRY. [2]

For the beginning lessons, the children "wait upon the directress." That is to say, they busy themselves in the opening days with many things indoors and out; they do not all advance upon the didactic material and make selections for use. Such a beginning would necessarily defeat its purpose, which is definite sense-training. When wise and convenient, the directress invites one child or another's attention to one of the

[1] Letters to a Mother, Blow. D. Appleton & Co.
[2] Special Method in Elementary Science. McMurry. The Macmillan Co.

simpler pieces of the apparatus. Others may watch
if they choose, may take turns if they become interested,
or may be given a different piece of apparatus. The
method is individual and in accordance with the three
periods of Seguin.

Typical Exercises.

   1. For Touch.

      (1.) First Period of Seguin.

         The sandpaper board is used. The directress
         says in distinct, well-modulated voice,
         "This is rough," "This is smooth" (lightly
         drawing the child's finger over the surfaces).
         (No unnecessary word is spoken to distract
         the child's attention or to confuse him.)

      (2.) Second period.

         With no interruption of the child's trend of
         thought, with no comment, the directress
         says, "Show me rough," "Show me smooth."

      (3.) Third period.

         After a brief time of silence, the directress
         leads to the final step by saying, "What is
         this?" Child answers, "Rough." "What
         is this?" Child answers, "Smooth." The
         child is then left with the material. If a child
         fails to respond satisfactorily, the teacher does
         not correct him or point out his error. Care
         is taken to see that the hands are clean.
         They are sometimes dipped in tepid water to
         make the sense more acute. Sight and touch
         are both used in the beginning in the recog-

nition of form.   Later, touch alone, or sight
alone are emphasized.

"Often after the introduction of such exercises it is a common
thing to have a child come to you, and closing his eyes touch with
great delicacy the palm of your hand or the cloth of your dress,
especially any silken or velvet trimmings." — MONTESSORI.

2. For Hearing.

(1.) This is loud.   (Shaking the box containing the
coarsest pebbles.)
This is soft.   (Shaking the box containing the
finest sand.)
Find the loud one.   Find the soft one.   Which
is this?   Which is this?

(2.) At another time a third box may be introduced.
This time the exercise may run: This is loud.
This is louder.   This is soft.

(3.) The eight pairs of boxes may be placed in order
so that there is perfect gradation from loud to
soft.

(4.) Duplicate sets of bells may be used.   The child
strikes one bell, then finds another which has a
corresponding tone.

(5.) A most valuable lesson in ear training as well as
bodily and spiritual poise is derived from the
game of Silence.   This exercise is so well
described by Dorothy Canfield Fisher that
she is quoted here at length.

"One exception to the general truth that the children in a
Montessori school do not take concerted action is in the 'lesson
of silence.'   It is certainly to visitors one of the most impressive
of all the impressive sights to be seen in the Children's Home.

"One may be moving about between the groups of busy children, or sitting watching their lively animation or listening to the cheerful hum of their voices, when one feels a curious change in the atmosphere like the hush which falls on a forest when the sun suddenly goes behind a cloud. If it is the first time one has seen this 'lesson,' the effect is startling. A quick glance around shows that the children have stopped playing as well as talking, and are sitting motionless at their tables, their eyes on the blackboard where in large letters is written 'Silenzio' (Silence). Even the little ones who cannot read follow the example of the older ones, and not only sit motionless, but look fixedly at the magic word. The Directress is visible now, standing by the blackboard in an attitude and with an expression of tranquillity which is as calming to see as the meditative impassivity of a Buddhist priest. The silence becomes more and more intense. To untrained ears it seems absolute, but an occasional faint gesture or warning smile from the Directress shows that a little hand has moved almost but not quite inaudibly, or a chair has creaked.

"At first the children smile in answer, but soon, under the hypnotic peace of the hush which lasts minute after minute, even this silent interchange of loving admonition and response ceases. It is now evident from the children's trance-like immobility that they no longer need to make an effort to be motionless. They sit quiet, rapt in a vague, brooding reverie, their busy brains lulled into repose, their very souls looking out from their wide, vacant eyes. This expression of utter peace, which I never before saw on a child's face except in sleep, has in it something profoundly touching. In that matter-of-fact, modern schoolroom, as solemnly as in shadowy cathedral aisles, falls for an instant a veil of contemplation, between human soul and the external realities of the world.

"And then a real veil of twilight falls to intensify the effect. The Directress goes quietly about from window to window, closing the shutters. In the ensuing twilight, the children bow their heads on their clasped hands in the attitude of prayer. The Directress steps through the door into the next room and a slow voice, faint and clear, comes floating back, calling a child's name. "'El . . . e . . . na!'

" A child lifts her head, opens her eyes, rises as silently as a little spirit, and with a glowing face of exaltation, tiptoes out of the room, flinging herself joyously into the waiting arms.

" The summons comes again, 'Vit . . . to . . . ri . . . o!'

PREPARING FOR THE GAME OF "SILENCE."

" A little boy lifts his head from his desk, showing a face of sweet, sober content at being called, and goes silently across the big room, taking his place by the side of the Directress. And so it goes until perhaps fifteen children are clustered happily about the teacher. Then, as informally and naturally as it began, the 'game' is over. The teacher comes back into the room with her usual quiet, firm step; light pours in at the windows; the mystic word is erased from the blackboard. The visitor is astonished to see that only six or seven minutes have passed since the beginning of this new experience. The children smile at each other, and begin to play

G

again, perhaps a little more quietly than before, perhaps more gently, certainly with the shining eyes of devout believers who have blessedly lost themselves in an instant of rapt and self-forgetting devotion." [1]

3. In the activity of weighing, the tablets are rested upon the palms, one in each hand, and weighed and grouped in piles according to their kind. The natural color of the wood makes this a self-corrective exercise, *i.e.* the child has taken the exercise without looking at the tablets; he now recognizes at a glance any errors he has made.

4. A beginning color exercise is that of matching, *i.e.*

> *a.* The colors are placed in a pile upon the table.
>
> *b.* A child is given a bright color from a duplicate set and asked to match it from the table.
>
> *c.* Later a number of tablets of differing tones of the same color are matched and arranged side by side with their duplicates on the table.
>
> *d.* More colors are introduced until the child can match all that are in the box and arrange them in their order.

Color Game. — Colors are piled on the table promiscuously. Each child is given one color with tints and shades. The game is to match these from the table, the group working together.

Testing Color Memory. — Show the child a color, then have him cross the room and select its match from a table.

5. In the exercise for the tactile-muscular sense the cubes and bricks are mixed and placed on the table be-

[1] A Montessori Mother, Dorothy Canfield Fisher, pp. 43–45.   Henry Holt & Co.

fore the child. After he becomes familiar with them his
eyes are closed and he places the cubes at the right side
and bricks at the left. Opening his eyes, he sees his own
errors if he has made them.

" These exercises of the stereognostic sense may be multiplied
in many ways. . . . They may raise any small objects — toy
soldiers, little balls . . . coins. They come to discriminate between small forms varying slightly such as corn, wheat and rice.
They are very proud of seeing without eyes, holding out their
hands and crying 'Here are my eyes, I can see with my hands !'"
— MONTESSORI.

In each case the directress tries to teach with con-
ciseness and simplicity, the particular lesson. She aims
to bring each new sensory experience to the child with a
minimum number of words and movements, thus con-
fining his attention to the central fact of the experience, *i.e.* a particular quality of a material object.
Upon the child's ability to grasp the lesson (make no
error) depends his continuance of the activity. The
teacher bases the next one in the series upon the ability
and upon the interest he shows; frequently this is made
manifest in specific requests to the teacher; at other
times, the mastery of previous exercises is taken as
evidence.

A kindergarten student recently attempted to teach
her niece of three by means of Seguin's lesson plan.
The result was as follows: This small relative, visiting
at her aunt's house, spied two brass candlesticks, one
containing a red candle, the other, a yellow candle.
The young aunt, thinking this an opportunity to apply her
new-found method, said to the child, pointing to the red

candle, "This is red"; pointing to the yellow candle, "This is yellow." The first step finished, she gave the second. "Show me red," "Show me yellow," to which the child responded. Feeling sure of the child's interest in the color, she went on to the third. "What is this?" pointing to the red candle. "This," said the child, "is a brass candlestick," bearing out Doctor Montessori's statement that the child's mind is apt to be confused regarding an object that has several striking characteristics.

It is believed that the spontaneous investigation of surroundings will come after the child has had such experiences as have been here described. He will apply his knowledge. A voluntary "explosion into the exploring spirit" comes as the natural result of the child's having had the object placed in his hand, of having his attention centered upon a particular aspect of it through the activity of some sense. He now transfers this evidence to other things within his environment, which, of course, should be a rich and varied one. Doctor Montessori says:

"We cannot create observers by saying, 'Observe,' but by giving children the power and the means for this observation, and these means are procured through education of the senses. Once we have aroused such activity, auto-education is assured, for refined, well-trained senses lead us to a closer observation of the environment, and this, with its infinite variety, attracts the attention and continues the psycho-sensory education."

Landscape gardening, schoolroom decoration and beautifully rendered, simple but good music must be counted upon as other sources of sensory experiences with educative values.

It would seem at first thought that the custom of placing all girls in aprons of one color and boys in aprons of another color and all on the same lines might be cutting off a vital source of sensory experience in general life — as uniformity in dress detracts from individuality. However, aprons placed on the children of the poor cover many discrepancies and make it possible for all to be clean and self-respecting. There are obvious reasons why the aprons might be of equal advantage to the overdressed children of the rich.

Observing the general happiness, intelligence and effectiveness of the little Montessori workers in the *good* schools in Rome, inspires faith in the didactic apparatus as valuable sensori-motor stimuli. But in considering the results achieved, one must keep in mind the general conditions which have made such success possible :

First. Desirable environment aside from the apparatus.

Second. The skillful scientific directress.

Third. The free, unhampered child.

To assume that such results can be secured by the use of the didactic materials without the conditions mentioned, is to overestimate their value and to belittle the principle and technique which give them their vitality and effectiveness. These materials will add an interesting and helpful feature in any home or school where there are young children, provided the mother or teacher is able to see them in their relationships to other things in the environment and other sources of education. Students of the method should be willing to make a thorough study of Doctor Montessori's book, bringing to it the sympathy and insight which will make possible (*a*) the gaining of her point of view, and (*b*) the measuring of that point of view by the best present-day standards, psychological, biological and social. Without this, the didactic materials for sense training will suffer the fate which the kindergarten materials have at times, when, in the hands of ignorant and untrained persons, they have proven valueless in nursery and school. The greatest drawback to the promotion of kindergarten interests in America has been the employment by school boards of incompetent, untrained so-called kindergarteners, on the supposition that "any one can teach small children." A community with such an ineffective worker soon decides that it does not care to continue its kindergarten, although knowing in reality no more about the real kindergarten than the small boy did about matrimony when he told his teacher he could not give a definition but knew that it was something his father and mother had had enough of.

The best friends of the Montessori method will be those who bring to its study the true Montessori spirit, which is that of the scientist who cares more for the truth than for systems as such, and who, while he is open-minded toward weaknesses, puts prejudice and sentimentality aside and recognizes all that is fundamental and desirable. In the consideration of this unique didactic material, there are naturally certain questions that arise.

First. In connection with the aspect of special sense-training, have animals, have men reached their present level of structural and functional sensory apparatus through special exercises, or through demands made upon them by efforts necessary for self-preservation, such as capturing or producing food, clothing and shelter?

An answer to this with a warning may be found in the following quotation from Dr. Earle Barnes.

"It is clear that before the child can live effectively he must arrange his stream of consciousness in series determined by use, form, size, color, smoothness or roughness, quantity, time, place, causation, or other qualities.

"With savages this arrangement of mental images largely waits on accidents of pain and pleasure.

"Things that please are selected and sought; things that offend are avoided. But with advancing intelligence, parental solicitude leads each generation to aid its children in making this arrangement quickly and effectively. Hence arises education.

"The most obvious way to assist the young, or the retarded minds of a later age, is to select samples belonging to one kind of serial arrangement, such as danger, desirability, use, form, color, time, language, or causation, and arrange them in a graded series which can be used as an exercise ground for the unformed mind. This mind is then led back and forth along this series until it gains the power to select and use the crude material of its daily experience after a similar pattern.

"Those interested in making these mental gymnasia are prone to grow so absorbed in their creations that after a time they forget that the justification for these exercising grounds is the aid they may give inexperienced minds in mastering the confused experience that makes up their real lives. To such compilers and teachers, the artificially arranged exercises become reality, and scholarship takes the place of living." [1]

This quotation from Dr. Barnes suggests two important points which we may apply in considering the didactic materials.

[1] Kindergarten Review, April, 1913. Report of Address. Dept. of Superintendence, N. E. A., 1913.

(1) Although the race has evolved its skill of sense discrimination through behavior with content and not formality, and although sensory content develops according to demands made for adjustment, for consistency in behavior, the parent or teacher may lead the child to a shorter cut in the educative process by giving repetitional experiences when memory is keen and habits are quickly formed.

(2) No material (Montessori or kindergarten) must be allowed to narrow the wide range of adjustments by taking the place of the rich sensory experiences, informal, unconventional, which the child may have when his own curiosity prompts him to discover how rough the chestnut burr is, or how velvety the moss. The story is told of the child who has been given many formal exercises for the recognition of the second gift, solids (sphere, cylinder and cube), and much training in looking for these forms in his surroundings. One day he exclaimed as he spied a dog on the street, "Oh, mother, see, there goes a long cylinder with four little cylinders under it, a cylinder sticking out behind it and a sphere in front of it."

With the free open courts and gardens, children in the Montessori schools do explore their environment and the school time is not all absorbed with the didactic apparatus. As used in these schools it does seem to fulfill her claim of helping in the formation of the habit of observation and of leading to the development of æsthetic taste and a natural interest in elementary science.

Second. Can a part of the brain be isolated from the rest of that organ for the sake of stimulating the activity and functioning of one sense? There is no doubt but that the closing of the eyes intensifies the impression through touch, but neurologists tell us that the absolute isolation of one sense is impossible. They also insist that sense gymnastics cannot bring about sense sharpening. Dr. Adolph Meyer is quoted as saying, "The word sense-training is a misnomer. It should be called attention and reaction training."

Third. Coupled with the didactic materials, should there be creative transformable stimuli which have the possibility of teaching the child processes and relationships? Should the repetitional exercises be joined with others which introduce unexpected and unusual situations for the child to meet? To quote the child study specialist, Elisabeth Ross Shaw:

"Professor Thomas says that the only difference between the mental efficiency of men and women is that men have been forced to form habits of reacting freely and swiftly to the emergencies of a swiftly moving environment (animals, enemies, machinery, etc.), while women have reacted to the more fixed environment of garden and house. He concludes that brain power is developed by the individual being forced to make swift, necessary movements, and that an environment is educative in proportion to the variety of its sudden hindrances in the carrying out of the individual's strongest purposes; thus stimulating his powers of invention and adaption. If this is true, no part of the educational system, from the Kindergarten up, can afford to ignore it." [1]

Fourth. Another question which comes to mind is this: Can mental power generated in one field be transferred to another? [2] Can the expert who handles and

[1] Address N. E. A., Salt Lake City, 1913.
[2] Education, Thorndike, p. 112–115. The Macmillan Co.

discriminates textures detect a counterfeit in paper money more quickly than the average man? Does the tea taster prove a better judge of wines because of his highly specialized training? Will the ability to memorize words or poems necessarily mean an equal ability to do the same with figures, dates, or mathematical formulæ? If it is true that the transfer is proportionate to the amount of identity between the practice field and the new field, and to the activity of an ideal of good working habits, is it important that all didactic material be used with a knowledge of this fact in order that results not attainable may not be looked for?

All the material should be used, with a knowledge that sensori-motor activity is most important, that the material meets spontaneously manifested needs during an early stage of child life and that it has therefore a definite contribution to make to child development. Especially is this true if the one who deals with this material is able to distinguish between the external name and physical equipment and that vital quality, embodied in principles intelligently worked out, which gives to any method its permanence and power.

QUESTIONS FOR DISCUSSION

1. In every school there are two types of children:
   (1) The sensory type; (2) the motor type. Give the characteristics of each type.
2. State the interrelation of impression and expression.
3. Why has expression in school work always lagged behind impression?

4. What natural instincts of childhood will act upon and react toward such materials as the didactic apparatus?

5. Make a comparative study of the educative use made of objects by Montessori, Froebel and Pestalozzi. Show the extent to which these uses seem to point to development along such lines as initiative, independence, imagination, creative effort, reasoning, judgment, organization of ideas, appreciation of the beautiful.

CHAPTER V

Writing, Phonics, Composition, Reading

THE spectacular feature of bursting into writing experienced by Montessori children has caught the public eye and tended to the overemphasis of a feature of the work which, though valuable in itself, is but a natural outgrowth of the fundamental ideas from which it springs.

The attention given this feature of the method is no doubt accounted for by our lack of satisfactory methods of teaching children to write. The slow, labored movements of the finger writing of the average child in expressing his own or another's thoughts on paper or blackboard, the muscular tension so apparent in this unnatural effort, with its reaction upon mental processes, makes us long for some means by which the child may master the mechanics of writing and revel in the enjoyment of this mode of expression with free, rapid and legible hand.

The plan herein described seems to point toward this goal, the following principles being taken into account :

1. The child should have gained power to execute before he is required to perform any task.

2. Eyesight in childhood is not accurate nor strong, hence overstrain should be avoided.

3. The sense of touch is keen and the child likes to reënforce sight and sound impressions by handling.

4. Two distinct elements are involved in writing, *i.e.* the holding of the pencil, the formation of the letters.

In short, Doctor Montessori's scheme is as follows. She aids the child to manipulate the pencil through work which she calls design. She teaches him the sounds of the letters and fixes these in his mind by means of visual, auditory and muscular memory. Then she teaches composition of words. The child is now ready to write the phonetic language and can compose any word he hears clearly pronounced.

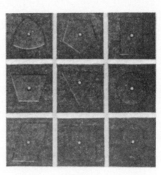

FIG. I.

The preparation begins with exercises in making designs of geometric figures, the object of which is to teach the child to manipulate the pencil.

Metal insets and their corresponding frames are used. (Fig. I.) These are placed upon little tables with sloping

FIG. 2.

tops. (Fig. 2.)

The child places a frame upon the paper and with a colored pencil which he has chosen traces around the empty center. Then he takes away the frame, finds the corresponding inset, places it upon the figure and draws around it with a pencil of different color. He then proceeds to fill in the outline.   At first the strokes are short and irregular, due to lack of muscular control.

Gradually the child becomes more skillful, and with longer and more sweeping movements produces lines nearly parallel, keeping well within the boundary of the

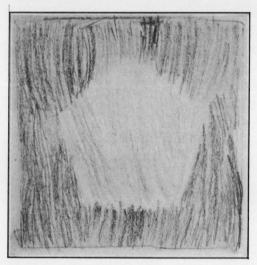

FIG. 3.

outline.   This, like other activities, is self-corrective in its tendency.   It develops into the more advanced step shown in Fig. 3.   Here the child not only outlines and fills in the central space, but fills in also the space made by drawing around the outer edge of the frame.   Later more difficult designs are made, Fig. 4.

"If we could count the lines made by a child in the filling in of these figures, and could transform them into the signs used in writing, they would fill many, many copy books!   Indeed, the security which our children attain is likened to that of children in the ordinary third elementary grade.   When for the first time our children take a pen or a pencil in hand, they know how to manage it almost as well as a person who has written for a long time." [1]

The next step is to associate the sound of a letter with visual and muscular tactile impressions, by the use of the single letters of the alphabet made of sandpaper and mounted on cards.

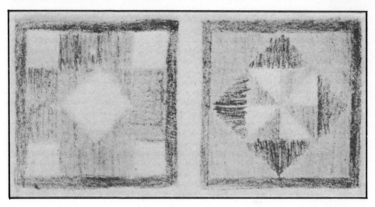

FIG. 4.

Using Seguin's lesson plan, the vowels are first introduced, followed by the consonants.

"This is '*a*'.   This is '*e*.'

" Touch '*a*'.   Touch '*e*.'

" What is this ?   What is this ?" [2]

The sound of the letter is given rather than the name, and a consonant sound is at once blended with some vowel with which the child is familiar.   Teaching *m* with *a*, one would say, "*m, a, ma*."   This lesson involves tracing — the child's index finger moving over the sandpaper letters as in writing, first with eyes open,

[1] The Montessori Method, p. 274.   [2] *Ibid.*, p. 276.

later with eyes closed, thus bringing into play the muscular tactile senses. The material is self-corrective,

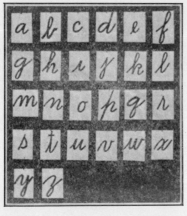

as the roughness of the letter and the smoothness of the card guide the fingers aright. (Fig. 5.)

The child is now ready for the composition of words. This is accomplished through the movable alphabet, the single letters of which are the same in dimension as the sandpaper letters and are placed in a box of compartments, the vowels being blue and the consonants pink. (Fig. 6.)

FIG. 5.

"It is most interesting indeed to watch the child at this work. Intensely attentive, he sits watching the box, moving his lips

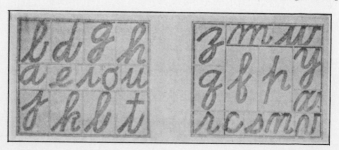

FIG. 6.

almost imperceptibly, and taking one by one the necessary letters, rarely committing an error in spelling. The movement of the lips reveals the fact that he repeats to himself an infinite number of times the words whose sounds he is translating into signs. Although the child is able to compose any word which is clearly pronounced, we generally dictate to him only those words which are well known, since we wish his composition to result in an idea. When these familiar words are used, he spontaneously rereads many times the word he has composed, repeating its sounds in a thoughtful, contemplative way." [1]

The preparation for writing is completed, yet Doctor Montessori does not request the child to try to write. This he eventually does, however. When one child starts, others follow. They can write any word they know by sound. This is where the American child is at a disadvantage. He cannot always tell how to spell a word by the way it sounds, and until our pioneers in simplified spelling give us English words which sound

[1] The Montessori Method, p. 283.

H

the same to the ear as they appear to the eye, we shall not, except with phonetic words, be able in America to make use of such a method as Doctor Montessori proposes — at least not without modifications.

In the training school of the Iowa State Teachers College some interesting results followed an experiment with this idea. An effort was made to carry out the plan of preparing for writing with as few modifications as possible. This was an easy task during the first two steps in the method, but when it came to the third — "The Composition of Words" — it was necessary to use great pains in selecting such words as were purely phonetic and at the same time familiar to the child. Added to these were some words from the lists given out by the Simplified Spelling Board. It was interesting to see with what delight the children composed these words with their cardboard letters. The entire method of procedure was something like this:

1. The work in design was carried out. This the children enjoyed heartily.

2. The sandpaper letters were introduced and traced, the three periods of Seguin being followed. Every attempt was made to provide a free, quiet atmosphere, conducive to attention. The tracing was done first with the forefinger, then with the fore and middle finger, then with the unsharpened end of a pencil, and finally in the air. Next, one child traced and another named the letter in a simple game.

3. Words were dictated and the children built them up with the movable alphabet. They were later encouraged to make any word they could spell. A game

developed in which one child would make a word and others would tell what it was.

The results were somewhat as follows :

1. The mastery of the crayon was acquired.

2. The children learned the names of the letters and how to write them in a short time. There was no element of drudgery.

3. The arm movement came easily and naturally and finger writing was not called into use.

4. Added interest and attention were given to the written form of words.

5. The work was in no way forced; on the contrary it was a continual source of interest and pleasure.

6. Children of their own accord used the colored crayons to write the words they knew.

7. The writing was legible from the first.

8. Growth came from voluntary action.

The following is an outline of this series of activities as described in " The Montessori Method." [1]

First Period.

1. *Purpose.*

> The purpose of the exercises is to develop the muscular mechanism necessary in holding and using the pen or pencil.

2. *Process.*

> The metal insets and their frames are taken by the child and used thus :

>> *a.* A metal frame is placed upon a sheet of paper and with a colored crayon the

[1] The Montessori Method, pp. 271-296.

child draws a line around the empty center; when the frame is taken away the child sees the figure in outline.

b. He then places the metal inset over the figure he has just drawn and follows the contour of this inset with a different colored crayon. When he lifts the metal inset he sees the same figure produced by two different pieces of apparatus.

c. The next step is the filling in of the figure. This work is continued until many and varied designs have been made.

3. *Result*.

Lines tend to stay within the outline, to become longer, more regularly placed, and evenly colored, showing that the child has established a number of definite coördinations which are involved in the control of a pencil.

Second Period.

1. *Purpose*.

The purpose of the exercise is to establish the visual-muscular images of the alphabetical signs and the muscular memory of the movements necessary to writing.

2. *Process*.

The single letters of the alphabet made of sandpaper and mounted on cards are used.

a. First Step.

The association of the visual, muscular and tactile images with letter *sounds*.

1. Using sandpaper vowel cards the directress sàys, "This is *a*," "This is *e*."

2. The child traces as he is shown the direction of movement by which the sounded letter is formed.

3. The child later traces with eyes closed, being guided by tactile and muscular impressions. For work by himself the child would doubtless be aided by having a line drawn under each letter; this would indicate the correct holding of the card.

b. Second Step.

The acquisition of visual, muscular, tactile images of letter *forms*.

The directress says "Give me *a*," "Give me *e*," thus encouraging the child to compare and recognize the letters when he hears the sounds corresponding to them.

If the child does not recognize the letters by sight, he traces them.

c. Third Step.

The mastery of the auditory image and the ability to give it *utterance* and apply it.

The directress, holding up the "*e*," says, "What is this?" The child responds, "*e*." "What is this?" "*a*."

3. *Results*.

First Step — The child has images of letter forms
and can make them.
Second Step — He has fixed the auditory image
of the letter.   He associates sound
with sign and points out the letter.
Third Step — He completes the letter mastery by
giving utterance to letter sounds.

Third Period.

1. *Purpose*.

The purpose is to utilize this letter mastery in the
building up of words.

2. *Process*.

By means of the use of letters cut out and classi-
fied in distinct sections of a box the child
arranges, on table or rug, the letters which
constitute familiar words.

The directress pronounces the word slowly and
distinctly, the child forms the word upon
the surface before him.[1]

Here again we find the possibility of self-correc-
tion, as after the word is placed the child
may sound it through and detect his own
errors.

This process consists of three steps:
a. The child selects his letters one by one from
the box.
b. He arranges these letters in form to represent
a word.

[1] The Montessori Method, p. 283.

    c. He puts the letters in their respective places
in the box, guided by the size of the compartments and by the letters which are
glued to the bottom of the same.

3. *Result.*

    By this practice there is a quickening of the
recognition of letter forms. Some day
the feeling and thought back of words
come forth, and the child writes, — he
bursts into writing that is legible from the
first.[1] The accompanying illustration
shows the various phases of the process
as follows: First child, at left and rear,
with box of letters. Second child, metal
frame, the table; exercise in design.
Third child, placing plane insets of wood
on cards. Fourth child, the first Seguin
step: "This is *a*." Fifth child, building letters into words. A child's delight
in the discovery of this new power is thus
described by Doctor Montessori.

"The child who wrote a word for the first time was full of excited joy. . . . Indeed, no one could escape from the noisy manifestations of the little one. He would call every one to see, and if
there was some one who did not go, he ran to take hold of their
clothes, forcing them to come and see.

"Usually this first word was written on the floor and then the
child knelt down before it in order to be nearer to his work and
contemplate it more closely. After the first word, the children
with frenzied joy continued to write everywhere. I saw children
crowding about one another at the blackboard, and behind the

[1] The Montessori Method, pp. 288–289.

MATERIALS LEADING TO WRITING AND READING.

little ones who were standing on the floor another line would form, consisting of children mounted upon chairs, so that they might write above the heads of the little ones. In a fury at being thwarted, other children, in order to find a little place where they might write, overturned the chairs upon which their companions were mounted. Others ran toward the window shutters or the door, covering them with writing. In these first days we walked upon a carpet of words." [1]

To aid in bringing together the results of these three periods of the process of writing, the following graph may be of use :

Control of instrument ⎤   ⎧ Phrases
Mastery of letter form ⎬ Process of writing ⎨ Sentences
Composition of letters ⎰   words   ⎩ Stories
   into words ⎭

The basic ideas underlying this plan for teaching writing are as follows :

1. The childish impulse for scribbling is directed into an activity having permanent value.

2. The muscular and tactile senses are very active in the early years. This results in the accumulation of a multitude of images which function later in interpreting quickly and accurately what is presented to the eye. Eyestrain is lessened through this use of the tactile-muscular mechanism.

3. Time, effort and nerve force are economized by a process which, quickly and without undue stimulation, produces happy, legible writers.

[1] The Montessori Method, p. 289.

Does this acquisition of writing contribute to other aspects of the mastery of verbal language?

Doctor Montessori maintains that it does. She conceives these definite relationships which may be stated as follows:

Composition. {
1. A discovery that words are composed of successive sounds that are blended together.
2. The building or spelling of words.
}

The phonetic element in the method contributes to *Reading* (Both silent and oral). {
Power of working out new words, both for pronunciation and for the gaining of ideas.
}

Composition and Reading.

{
A discovery that written forms can convey interesting ideas.

Habit of correct articulation, of natural and varied inflections and pleasing voice qualities.
}

Doctor Montessori's recognition of the interrelation between aspects of verbal language is not foreign to recent discussions of the teaching of reading, writing and composition. Professor Percival Chubb has expressed it thus :

"Our basic conception, be it remembered, is that the process of learning to use one's mother tongue to good effect in speaking and writing it, and to appreciate and catch inspiration from its master-products ought to be regarded as a single organic process, each stage of which must be seen in relation to those that precede and follow." [1]

There is not identity in all that is involved in the treatment of this problem by these two educators. Decided differences are found in the approach to, and in the emphasis upon, the form and content sides.

The contributions that writing makes to composition have already been referred to. To one who has observed the children's interest and ease in oral and written composition, it seems strange that Doctor Montessori should not have given more space to the treatment of this topic in her book. From it one sees that conversation about "what the children have done the day before, the intimate happenings of the family, games, public

[1] The Teaching of English, Chubb, p. 19.   The Macmillan Co.

THE MUCH-FAMED WRITING.

The materials and methods which result in legible, uniform writing without strain.   Via Giusti School.

happenings, birthday parties, etc.," [1] is encouraged.   In
telling these experiences the children would have practice
in narration, description and explanation, — three
recognized forms of composition.   In addition to this,
their taste concerning suitable topics would be developed.
The teacher aims consciously, in tactful ways, to eliminate tendencies towards the discussion of home affairs
that should be kept private and other matters that
are unpleasant or valueless.   An experience described [2]
is evidence that written composition is not ignored in
practice; it shows that the children moved into composition spontaneously because the two preparatory
steps had been taken.   They had expressed their ideas
orally; they had acquired the mechanics of writing.
It was therefore natural that several of a group rose
during a free conversation period, "and with expres-
sions of joy on their faces ran to the blackboard and
wrote phrases on the order of the following: 'Oh,
how glad we are that our garden has begun to bloom !' "
This type of activity proved as fascinating as did the
previous spontaneously acquired ones.   The children
were busy for days writing sentences about their experiences.   Several sentences, on the same experience, were
forthcoming.   Special occasions called for more elaborate compositions.   The letters written at Christmas and
Easter time, and greetings to visitors, are examples.

   To follow the line of work which the Montessori
Method stands for in composition, one would count on
(1) the preparatory steps having been taken in the
phonetic and manual phases of the writing process;

---

[1] The Montessori Method, p. 124.   [2] *Ibid.*, p. 304.

(2) the descriptive, narrative and explanatory elements in conversation dealing with children's experiences, and (3) the same elements in the written form.

On the relationships of written composition to reading, another aspect of the mastery of the language arts, Doctor Montessori places emphasis.[1] She maintains that it forms the transition between enjoyment of the mechanical and the thought-gaining phases of reading. In fact, before the child will read for sense, he must discover that groups of written words are not merely arrangements of letters having sounds and standing for things in his environment, but that they convey his ideas to some one else, or *vice versa*.[1]

Before this discovery is made the child has had placed before him cards upon which are written in large, clear script some words which have already been pronounced by the child and which represent objects with which he is familiar. Furnishings for a doll's house, balls, trees, tin soldiers and railways are typical of the objects that are used. Long and short words are pronounced with equal ease, as the child already knows how to pronounce any word or the sounds that compose it. He is at once permitted to " translate the written word into sounds." If these are correctly given, the directress says, "Faster." The child repeats them more rapidly, but often does not yet comprehend them. "Faster, faster," says the directress. " The child reads faster, each time repeating the same accumulation of sounds, with increasing speed, until the word bursts upon his consciousness and he pronounces it."[2] This is con-

[1] The Montessori Method, pp. 303–307.   [2] *Ibid.*, p. 298.

tinued for some time.   The exercise is varied by having the card carried to, and placed under, the object it names. The correct reading of the card entitles the child to the use of the toy or object.   The toys are soon put aside by the children, however, in favor of the reading of *many* cards.

Now, all the elements that constitute reading for thought have been experienced and the child is ready for the sentence.   The action sentences, so familiar to the primary teacher, are introduced.   They are placed on blackboards and on large cards and smaller slips of paper in both the script and printed forms.   These are followed by the reading of larger units,—accounts of the actual observations and experiences of the children in their immediate environment.   This material is prepared by the teacher upon sheets of paper.   Doctor Montessori, with others, has found that the average first reading books do not meet the requirements of a really developing method.   When this teacher-made reading material is to be supplemented or supplanted by the market-made books, is determined by the one in charge.   The children's spontaneous interest in such books would influence this decision.   Much of the reading of action sentences and of leaflets is silent reading.

In considering the theory upon which this method is based, it may be well to recall the complete process.

Letters.
1. Hearing sounds.
2. Association of sounds with letter forms.   { Sand paper letters.
3. Making sounds associated with letter forms.

Words.	1. Recalling sounds, selecting corresponding letter forms from the box.	Boxes of movable alphabets.
	2. Building sounds into words.	
	3. Connecting words with objects.	Word cards and miscellaneous objects.
	4. Oral reading of individual words.	Cards, slips of paper.
Sentences and Larger Units.	1. Discovery that words convey thought.	Blackboard, paper and pencil.
	2. Reading groups of words for thought (chiefly silently).	Leaflets, books.

Some of the basic reasons given for the use of this method of reading are :

1. Beginning early is essential. Muscular and tactile senses are responsive then and the vocal mechanism plastic. Habits of poor articulation, voice quality and inflection have not been established. All who visit the Montessori schools with some knowledge of the liquid Italian tongue are charmed with the soft mellow voices of the children as well as the musical inflection and rhythmic flow of their speech, the articulation, accent and enunciation seeming to be almost perfect. This is due in part to temperamental and climatic causes, but in a larger measure to accurate training.

2. The contributions from other and preceding activities are utilized. The method leads from design through spelling, writing and composition to reading. The training of the muscles of the hand, the exercises in articulation and enunciation, the discipline of the memory, the gaining of mental images, — all are out of the way before the child is expected to really read. This is probably the explanation of Doctor Montessori's statement that "we should find the way to teach the child *how* before making him execute a task." [1]

If one is liberal in the interpretation of the word "task," her thinking would seem to be in line with that of Hughes:

"It may be laid down as a fundamental law that when a child or a man is asked to perform any complex operation, he should be able to give his direct or primary attention to the highest element, or stage, in the complex process. The processes subordinate to the highest should be so thoroughly under his control that he can perform them automatically, or without conscious effort. When a child is expressing thought in writing, for instance, he should not be required to think about the forms of the letters. Letter formation should have become automatic, or else the child must give a portion of his mental effort to the construction of the letters, and he will have only a part of his mind left to do his thinking. If a man is able to concentrate his mind fully on his subject while writing, he cannot be conscious of the fact that there are letters or words, or grammatical rules, or laws of style. He thinks, and the language is organized, and the visible words formed, without direct conscious effort on his part." [2]

3. Silent reading is to precede, and to receive as much attention as oral reading.

[1] The Montessori Method, p. 261.
[2] Teaching to Read, James L. Hughes, p. 4.   The A. S. Barnes Co.

I

"Reading aloud implies the exercise of two mechanical forms of the language — articulate and graphic — and is, therefore, a complex task and one of the most difficult intellectual actions. The child, therefore, who begins to read by interpreting thought should read mentally." [1]

This attitude toward the place and amount of silent reading is familiar to students of McMurray, Huey, Briggs and Coffman, Gesell, and others. These authors see in the oral reading, early and excessive, one cause of artificial expression and of some cases of stuttering.

There is no doubt but that so-called expression in the early grades is much overdone.

" The Director of Physical Training in the Boston Public Schools, after careful investigations, tells us that the elementary schools are 'the breeding ground' of the stuttering habit, and that stuttering 'is largely due to faulty and misguided instruction in speaking and reading.' " [2]

This completes the discussion of Doctor Montessori's Method of teaching the language arts. She consciously makes the approach from the form side, expecting a mastery of this mechanical phase before attempting to solve the thought problem. From that approach, the plan is consistent throughout and in use reaches the goal sought. This is evident to any one who has visited The Children's Houses, or has experimented intelligently with the method elsewhere.

The opposite approach, made from the standpoint of motivation, was emphatically brought forward by Colonel Parker, some twenty years ago. It has influ-

[1] The Montessori Method, p. 107.
[2] The Psychology and Pedagogy of Reading, Huey, p. 352. The Macmillan Co.

enced the views of the teaching of these arts held by leading American educators since that time. Books written by authors referred to here embody the resulting methods.

TOPICS FOR DISCUSSION

Give your views on the following:

1. Artificial expression in reading in relation to
    a. Poor voice quality.
    b. Dependence upon others for interpretation.
2. Silent and oral reading: their relative values in life experience.
3. The importance of giving early attention to defects in speech.
4. The value as a preparation for written composition of
    a. Dramatization in connection with story-telling and every day activities.
    b. Free spontaneous conversation.
    c. A wealth of joyous experience.
5. The relative values of the methods and materials used in teaching reading by Doctor Montessori in the Casa dei Bambini, Rome; and Flora J. Cook, in the Francis W. Parker School, Chicago.[1]

[1] Course of Study, Francis W. Parker School, Vol. I, No. II, 1913. Also Reading in the Primary Grades, Flora J. Cook.

CHAPTER VI

THE number instinct is strong in every normal child. Long before the school period, even before his use of spoken language for his counting one, two, three, the child rhythmically touches the objects within his reach, saying syllables which indicate a consciousness of the fewness or multiplicity of things. He sits for an hour at a time shifting the sand in his sand pile from one place to another, measuring and counting by pailfuls with the greatest satisfaction. He enjoys the process of arranging sticks, pebbles and cards into bundles or groups, thus playing himself into a kind of number experience, which, though vague and crude, forms the basis of his later mathematical education. This number instinct, so active as to cause the child to observe, compare and classify, is turned to such account by Doctor Montessori that by the use of suitable stimuli hazy notions of number soon begin to grow into definite number facts, and the child, through a knowledge of processes and units of measure, comprehends with some degree of definiteness the objects and activities within his environment on their quantitative side. This gives him added power to see, to think and to do.

Montessori would begin her teaching of numeration by the use of familiar objects.

"A dozen different ways may serve toward this end and daily life presents many opportunities; when the mother says, for instance, 'There are two buttons missing from your apron,' or 'We need three more plates on the table.'" [1]

The tower, the broad stair and the long stair offer many suggestions for the mother, kindergartner and primary teacher. The tower offers opportunity for indefinite comparison. The broad stair teaches thickness. The long stair emphasizes the idea of length, and leads definitely to counting and measuring. (See cuts, page 72.) The sandpaper and cardboard figures give the written forms of the numbers and are much used in games and undirected work. From these the child moves into the making of his own written forms on blackboard and paper.

The suggestions for the use of these devices grow out of the study of the chapter on The Teaching of Numeration; [2] the observation of children's work in the schools in Rome; and some experiments with American children. An attempt has been made to carry the work beyond that specifically described in the Montessori Method without, however, indicating the age at which the child should have it. This must be determined by the child's interest in, and capacity for, the work, and the suitableness of such material for his stage of growth.

"Each teacher may multiply the practical exercises in the arithmetical operations, using simple objects which children can readily handle and divide." [3]

[1] The Montessori Method, p. 326.
[2] Ibid., Chapter XIX.   [3] Ibid., p. 337.

I. Indefinite Comparison.

(a) (Type of the early exercises.)   Use the tower.
The teacher says:
This is a small block (smallest block).
This is a large block (largest block).

Show me the large block.
Show me the small block.

What is this?   (Points to one.)
What is this?   (Points to the other.)
Later exercise.
The teacher says:
This is a large block.
This is a larger block.   (Shows only 2 blocks.)
This is the largest block here. (Shows 3
blocks.)

Bring the large block.
Bring the block that is larger.
Bring the largest block.

Which block is this?   (Points to largest one.)
Which block is this?   (Points to large one.)
Which block is this?   (Puts largest aside and
with other two present, points to larger one.)
Leave the child with these blocks. Observe
what he does with them.
Teach: Small, smaller, smallest.

(b) Use the broad stair.
Teach: Thick, thin —

Thick, thicker, thickest.
Thin, thinner, thinnest.

Narrow, wide —
    Narrow, narrower, narrowest.
    Wide, wider, widest.

(c) Use the long stair.
    Teach : Long, short —
        Long, longer, longest.
        Short, shorter, shortest.

THE TOWER AND THE LONG STAIR.

Other comparisons will suggest themselves with the groups of materials named in (a), (b), (c).

The exercises should increase in difficulty. Children

as well as adults enjoy overcoming greater and greater obstacles; enjoy testing and measuring their abilities. These can grow only as attempts are made upon the more difficult. One such variation is suggested; others will come as materials are used by children and teacher. The step of "Bring me the . . . block," will at first show the blocks near each other; later, they can be placed at greater distances; and finally in different parts of the room. Here the child cannot glance back and forth at the objects but must use the memory image as his test in selection.

The final goal in this work of indefinite comparison is reached when each series of blocks can be placed in order of gradation without error and with speed. It is to be borne in mind that these materials are self-corrective; they stimulate the child to judgment of his own work; they lead to self-direction.

There is a valuable language training in such exercises as these. The defining and classifying of experiences and the acquisition of a vocabulary expressing the same are related processes. In this case the child unconsciously gains a foundation for the comprehension of the real force and meaning of that phase of technical grammar, the comparison of adjectives.

II. Definite Number Work.

(I)   Teaching number content and the "graphic sign."

For definite number work with the long stair, the child arranges the scattered rods in order, according to their length, being aided by the correspondence of colors.

This is another exercise that is self-corrective, and the child, verifying his own work,
takes additional steps toward self-help.

The first lesson, as Doctor Montessori[1]
presents it, is to have the child place
the rods correctly. Having done this, he
counts the spaces, the red and blue,
always beginning with the smallest one.
For example, he touches the rod of one
decimeter and counts, "One." Then
touches the next longer and says, "One,
two," etc., always going back to *one* and
starting from the side having the larger
number of spaces.

The next step is to name the rods from
the shortest to the longest, according to
the spaces, touching the rods at the side
which make the stair. The spaces in the
longest rod are counted both from left
to right, and right to left. Here the principle of verification is again operative.
The triangular arrangement of the long
stair makes it possible for the child to
count to ten on all three sides. He counts
the stairs going up and down, as in the
first lesson, thus learning the number of
spaces in all of the different rods. Counting from the top to the bottom and
vice versa on the shortest side of the triangle, he discovers the number of rods.

[1] The Montessori Method, p. 193.

He learns the number of spaces in the longest rod by counting the red and blue sections on the other side of the triangle. The results have been the same as when the longest rod was counted — 1, 2, 3, 4, 5, 6, 7, 8, 9, 10.

Exercises are now given in which the child selects rods of different lengths. For example, the directress says, "Show me five," and the child points to the rod having the five sections. He verifies it by placing two rods side by side and counting their sections, thus learning to combine, or group. The child has by this time learned to assign a particular name to each one of the spaces in the long stair, and now the spaces may be called piece number *one*, piece number *two*, etc., and later, *one*, *two*, etc. All the rods are treated as was the " 5," hence the combinations to ten are made.

When the child has learned to identify and call each rod by name, it is time to teach him the figure or symbol of the number content, which Doctor Montessori terms the "graphic sign." This involves connecting the familiar audible form of the sign with the unfamiliar visible form. The manner of presenting this is similar to that used for teaching the letters, colors, etc. The material

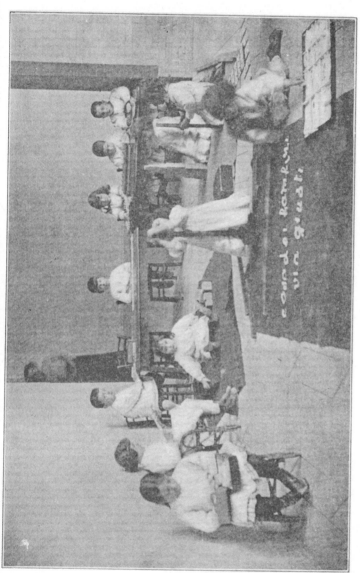

THE TOWER, THE BROAD STAIR, THE LONG STAIR, THE SOLID INSETS AND THE COUNTING CASE ARE IN EVIDENCE.

The child in the foreground is arranging words from the alphabet boxes.

is the cards with sandpaper figures.   For
example:

This is seven.
This is three.

Give me three.
Give me seven.

Which is this?
Which is this?

As the child is dealing with these
cards, he is asked to place them against
the rods of the long stair.   This strength-
ens the ties of association between the
written and the oral forms of the symbol
and their content.   The two trays, each
divided into five compartments, and the
counting sticks are then used with these
same cards.   The first tray has the cards
with — o, 1, 2, 3, 4, — and the second —
5, 6, 7, 8, 9, — placed in order in the
sections (Fig. 1).   The counting sticks

FIG. 1.

are not in the box.   The exercise consists
in putting them in the compartments in
the groupings and order designated by the
figures on the cards placed in the box.

When the child asks how many objects he shall put into the zero section, the meaning of that term is explained. But this is not sufficient to impress it upon him. Several other devices are used; among them are:

(1) "Come to me zero times."

(2) "Take zero steps."

(3) Games may be played with cards upon which are the figures 0, 1, 2, 3, 4, 5, 6, 7, 8, 9. The children take, bring or do the number of things which cards they draw call for.[1]

(II) The fundamental processes.

Numbers below ten:

(A) Counting.

(B) Addition.

$$
\begin{array}{ccccc|cccc}
(1)\ 9 & 8 & 7 & 6 & 5 & 1 & 2 & 3 & 4 \\
1 & 2 & 3 & 4 & 5 & 9 & 8 & 7 & 6 \\
\hline
10 & 10 & 10 & 10 & 10 & 10 & 10 & 10 & 10
\end{array}
$$

Making other rods the same length as "10." "What did you put with nine to make ten? Tell it with the number cards." "Show it with these (pebbles, cubes, etc.) objects." Teacher points to eight and two. "What have we here? Make it with the number cards."

[1] The Montessori Method, pp. 329–330.

"With these objects." All the other combinations making ten may be treated in the same way.

(2) "We can do with nine what we did with ten," etc.

$$
\begin{array}{cccc} \quad \quad \begin{array}{cccc}
8 & 7 & 6 & 5 \\
\underline{1} & \underline{2} & \underline{3} & \underline{4} \\
9 & 9 & 9 & 9
\end{array} \quad \quad \begin{array}{cccc}
1 & 2 & 3 & 4 \\
\underline{8} & \underline{7} & \underline{6} & \underline{5} \\
9 & 9 & 9 & 9
\end{array}
\end{array}
$$

(3) "What rod would you like to use to-day?" Child chooses. It may be six, five or any of the remaining ones. The children should be encouraged to show many combinations with objects other than the rods.

(4) The preceding combinations may be worked out from another standpoint, for the sake of fixing them in the child's mind, by using the rods in the following manner.

(a) Adding one to other numbers, using the rods, we discover these facts:

$$
\begin{array}{cccccccc}
2 & 3 & 4 & 5 & 6 & 7 & 8 & 9 \\
\underline{1} & \underline{1} & \underline{1} & \underline{1} & \underline{1} & \underline{1} & \underline{1} & \underline{1}
\end{array}
$$

(b) Adding two:

$$
\begin{array}{cccccccc}
1 & 2 & 3 & 4 & 5 & 6 & 7 & 8 \\
\underline{2} & \underline{2} & \underline{2} & \underline{2} & \underline{2} & \underline{2} & \underline{2} & \underline{2}
\end{array}
$$

(c) Adding three:

I	2	3	4	5	6	7
<u>3</u>	<u>3</u>	<u>3</u>	<u>3</u>	<u>3</u>	<u>3</u>	<u>3</u>

(d) Other combinations may be made by adding:

4, 5, 6, 7, 8.

(C) Subtraction.

The work in subtraction need not be left until all the combinations in addition have been worked out. It is not planned out in full here, for in general it will follow the same course as the work in addition.

Type lesson. "Make as many tens as possible." "What rods did you put together in this one?" (Points to nine and one combination.) "Let us take it apart now." "Let us tell what we have done. Ten less one, nine. Let us tell it with these (pebbles, etc.) objects. This is the way it looks on the board:" 10

$$\frac{-\ 1}{9}$$

"Make it with your number cards."

(D) Addition and subtraction. Exercises
with numbers below ten :

(1) Teaching + and − signs. Material :
Sandpaper signs mounted on
cards to correspond to figure
cards. Use the three steps of
Seguin. "These are to tell us
when to put together" and when
to "take apart." "Which
one do you think says, 'put
together'?" (Since the plus
sign is a "putting together"
of two lines, the child will
probably make correct selection. "Then which one is the
'take apart' one?" "The
chalk will tell you to do some
'putting together' and 'taking apart' with your rods.

(2) "To-day, we will use the rods and
other things. You may tell
with the number and sign cards
what I do."

(3) Other lessons fixing the process and
extending the mastery of the
combinations up to ten will
suggest themselves.

(4) When ready, the children should
substitute the making of the
figures with crayon at board or
on paper for the use of the

number and sign $(+, -)$ cards to tell what has been done with rods and other objects or pictures of them.

(5) The final step involves the elimination of the objects or representations of them. The use of a problem on board and cards at this stage should aim to have the child give result as quickly as he can without naming the numbers that are to be added. The automatic response to,

$$2 \quad 4 \quad 3 \quad 7$$
$$+3 \quad +3 \quad -2 \quad -2$$

etc., should be 5; 7; 1; 5; respectively. It should not be the more drawn out form of "$2 + 3 = 5$." The good accountant does not waste time and energy in saying five words where one will do. The one-word habit cannot be established too early.

(I) & (II) Continued with numbers above ten.

(a) Review zero devices. "Place 'ten' and 'one' (rods) together. This makes eleven. We have no more figures with which to make eleven, so we put the card containing '1' over the

K

zero (counting frame, Fig. 2),
and then we have eleven.
Write eleven on the board."

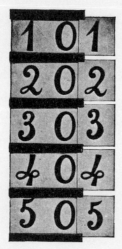 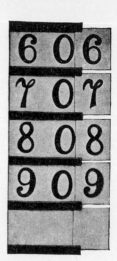

FIG. 2. — THE COUNTING FRAMES.

"Place 'ten' and 'two' together. This makes twelve.
Here is twelve (with the
number cards). I put the
card containing '2' over the
zero. Then we have the
number twelve. Write
twelve on the board below
eleven."

"Place 'ten' and 'three'
together. This is thirteen.
Ten and three make thir-
teen. Make it in the num-

ber case. Write it on the board," etc.

The meaning of and the graphic sign for fourteen, fifteen, sixteen, seventeen, eighteen and nineteen, may be worked out in the same way with the rods.

The combinations making eleven, twelve, thirteen and fourteen, fifteen, sixteen, seventeen, eighteen, may be developed in addition and subtraction until the child has them up to 20.

(b) Counting.

(1) By 1's to 20 and reverse.

(2) By 2's to 20 and reverse. Teacher takes out every other rod, beginning with two and places them in order for the child. Child names the rods, beginning with the smallest, — 2, 4, 6, 8, 10. "Count up this stair. Count down. Count up and down." "Notice what blocks have been left. Name them." (1, 3, 5, 7, 9.) "Count up and down as many times as

you like." Vary with ob-
jects. Eliminate objects
when no longer necessary.

(3) Other countings. With and without objects.

(a) By 3's to 18 and reverse.

(b) By 4's to 20 and reverse.

(c) By 5's to 20 and reverse.

(4) By 10's to 100 and reverse. "Climb
up the stair (rods) counting
each step, calling the first
step 10. Climb down.
Climb up and down."

(5) The use of the counting trays and
sticks and the counting frame
and figure cards make it possible to teach counting up to
100. The specific steps involved in counting by 1's,
2's, 10's, etc., beyond the
limits suggested by (b) under (I) and (II) will suggest
themselves to the worker
with children as the latter
manifest their needs and
their readiness.

(c) Multiplication.

(1) Type lesson. Table of 2's. Count
by 2's to 20. Find rods 2, 4,
6, 8, etc. Hold up rod 2.
How many times do you see 2

in this block? 1 time.
1 times 2 = 2.

Teacher writes   2
$$\times 1$$
2

Bring rod 4. Turn 2 on 4 to find
how many times you do it.
2 times 2 = 4. Teacher
writes   2
$$\times 2$$
4

See if you can find a block that will
contain 2, three times. 3
times 2 = 6. Teacher writes

2
$$\times 3$$
6

Treat each step similarly.

Use the counting sticks to review,
and fix process and extend
the multiplication combinations. Use the number cards
and the times sign to have
child record the results.
Eventually, have him write
the results when he works
with objective material.
Follow this with the elimination of all objects and the
fixing of the desired response
to:

$$\begin{array}{cccc} 2 & 2 & 4 & 3 \\ \times\,4 & \times\,3 & \times\,2 & \times\,2 \end{array}$$

etc., with 8, 6, 8, 6, respectively. Then, miscellaneous problems for quick and accurate response to the three signs, $+$, $-$, $\times$, should be given for testing, reviewing and fixing the correct association of processes with these symbols.

(d) Division.

(1) Type lesson. "Divide four by two. That means put 2 on four and see how many times it will go into four. How many 2's in four? Here it is on the board, $4 \div 2 = 2$." Develop each division fact after this fashion and follow the general scheme of progress suggested in processes already discussed.

(2) Type lesson in fractioning. "We find one half of anything by cutting it or dividing it into two equal parts. Let us find one half of two, four, six, eight and ten. We will use this cord to show where to divide. Take rod 'two.' Cut

it into two equal parts with the cord. Show one half of 'two' by running your finger along it. How many is it? This is the way to write it: $\frac{1}{2}$ of $2 = 1$." Develop $\frac{1}{2}$ of 4; $\frac{1}{2}$ of 6; etc., in a like manner.

(e) That the long stair offers many and varied experiences with numbers is evident. Another aspect not yet referred to is that it embodies the units of the metric system.

Our remote ancestors did their counting by the aid of the ten fingers. It seems natural to divide numbers into groups of tens. By making the longest rod one meter and the shortest rod one decimeter, Doctor Montessori brings to the child a basis of measurement which is destined in time to become universal.

In the metric system, the unit of length is the meter; the unit of capacity, the liter; the unit of weight, the gram. Each table contains in an unvarying ratio multiples and decimals of its unit, and hence is simpler to acquire and apply than the non-metric systems. At present there are only a few statements in each table that are in common usage. In some schools are to be found the rulers, scales, etc., for the measurement of length, weight and capacity, according to the metric system. They are all needed for frequent use by children when the "measuring more exactly" interest is active. Furniture and people; pebbles and sand; water and sand, are

BUILDING WITH THE TOWER AND THE BROAD STAIR.

Children are free to carry their rugs and materials to any place they choose.

some of the things to which may be applied the appropriate meter, or the gram, or liter measures. It is only a step for the child to construct his own instruments of linear measure out of paper, for by placing the longest rod upon paper, drawing around it and then cutting out, he has his own tape line or ruler. Folding this into ten equal parts he has sections which are decimeters and the equivalent in length of the red and blue sections on the longest rod. Again, if he folds the decimeter into ten, he has sections which are one centimeter in length, and if it were best for a small child to do such fine work, he could fold a centimeter into ten sections, and make the length of the millimeter. This experience might suggest to the child the dividing of a gram of sand into the smaller and smaller groups of tens or into divisions that constitute the units of the weight measure. The efforts at measuring and of making the units of measure would fix the nature of the decimal system indelibly in the child's mind, both on its multitude and on its magnitude sides. Such work should be followed by exercises in which the child estimates length, weight and capacity, by looking, or by looking and lifting. Having passed the judgment that the "table is two meters away," he should verify the same with ruler or rod; having gauged the weight of a "package at three grams," he should place it on scales to determine the accuracy of his statement.

So far, experiences with the metric system have been confined to the basis unit and its subdivisions. Others, dealing with the multiples of the same, should also be arranged for as the child is ready for them, thus completing the work with the system.

In studying the development of our best methods, we find that Pestalozzi gave the first impetus to logical elementary number work by recognizing the value of perception and the use of objects in training the number sense. His pupil, Grube, followed him with the theory that all of the combinations of a number should be taught a child simultaneously by means of objects. This proved to be impracticable, as a clear idea of process should go hand-in-hand with figures and number facts.

Froebel urged that the child should not only see and handle objects in connection with numerical ideas, but that the process should be consciously applied by the handling of materials creatively, thus harmonizing number with his law of inner connection and illustrating the fact that while the child works or plays, quite unconscious of numerical combination, fundamental number truths may be mastered.

Modern American methods are somewhat influenced by the work of these early reformers, although many modifications have developed. These have culminated in such logical treatises as "Special Method in Number," by McMurry; "The Psychology of Number," by McLellan and Dewey; and for children's use, such books as "First Journeys in Numberland," by Stone and Harris, and "Primary Arithmetic," by Smith.

The importance attached to motivation and activity in number teaching is suggested by McMurry, who says:

"Dr. Dewey bases the development of the number idea upon measurement, and measurement implies activity — the adjustment of means to an end. The number one is not a fixed thing, but a standard unit with which to measure some larger yet undefined whole." "This appeal to activity in measuring by means of standard units we consider to be a sounder basis for the number concept than mere observation as practiced by Pestalozzi."

Probably the manner of teaching number most frequently compared with that of Montessori is the Speer method. This method is based, in the main, on sound principles, and has left a permanent influence upon methods of teaching number, though losing its identity as a system. Its author considered the fundamental thing in arithmetic to be the inducing of judgment of relative magnitudes. Because it is the relation of things that makes them what they are, he brought these relations to the child by repeated acts of comparison. He did not believe in building up a whole which the child had never seen, but would have the mind grasp the whole first, then move to its parts, *i.e.* a conception of four is necessary before developing the number fact $2 + 2$, 4. It was Speer's idea to place materials within the child's reach, allowing him to handle, measure and compare before interfering with questions or directions. He offers many exercises by which the child gains familiarity through the senses of touch, and sight, with simple geometric solids, planes and lines.

This idea holds the child to much preliminary work in comparing and measuring before giving him number facts, and this is a good idea. Possibly its devotees carried it to extremes, as the plan with all its details seemed to prove too elaborate, holding the child so closely to concrete forms that he was unable to think processes in the absence of objects.

The Montessori method is quite different from that of Speer. She has a smaller variety of solid forms, her materials are self-corrective, she makes greater use of the sense of touch and she goes quickly from the exercise in comparison to the teaching of number facts and relations. In her system, more undirected work is practiced by the children and the lessons are given to individuals rather than to groups.

TOPICS FOR DISCUSSION

1. What part does observation play in number development?
2. Give incidental work in arithmetic in connection with:
   a. Nature study.
      (1) Weather records.
      (2) Plant life.
   b. Construction Work.
      (1) Measuring.
      (2) Wholing and parting.
   c. Reading.
      (1) Finding pages.
      (2) Finding sections.
3. How may number facts and processes be made usable by much application and practice?
4. Discuss the relation of motivation to clear mathematical reasoning.
5. Discuss the relation of repetition and drill to accuracy and speed in arithmetical work.
6. What relation is there between number development and

a. Neatness of arrangement.

b. Accuracy of expression.

c. Clearness of thought.

7. Make a comparative outline of the methods and materials used in teaching arithmetic in

a. The Casa dei Bambini, Rome.

b. The Speyer School, New York.

(See the Speyer School Curriculum, 1913.)

CHAPTER VII

THE child's hand as a means for expressing his inner life has been the subject of many studies, and the data given to us by Hall, Preyer and other psychologists show the significance of the activities of this small dimpled member of the child's body which tells the drift of his interests, the scope of his initiative and the power of his inventive impulses. These are also expressed through speech and through games and plays. But the things done with the hand have a peculiar interest to one who has the insight to catch their hidden meaning.

It may be that the squirrel molded in clay is many times too large for the hollow log which he is supposed to enter; that the house drawn on the blackboard not only shows doors and windows, but interior as well, imagination causing the wall to be accommodatingly transparent; that the landscape produced by washes with brush and paint reveals impossible colorings in grass and sky: each crude effort has wrapped up in it, nevertheless, a fascinating story of a child's vague wonderings, tastes and ideas. At the beginning the primary value of all activities of the hand is self-expression; a secondary one is their preparatory aspect.

Technique, which is only a means to an end, is gradually acquired through experience and training.[1]

It is most important that by the means of such mediums as clay, sand and crayon the child shall clarify his ideas by putting them into visible form, acquire the habit of expressing thoughts freely with different mediums, associate hand and eye through motor activity, and tell the uppermost thoughts of the moment with absolute freedom and satisfaction.

"The external organ (hand) has been accordingly more employed to utter and set forth the movement of the internal organ (mind) than any other outward part of the body." [2]

The activities of the hand of the individual run parallel with those of the race. Just as the child by means of the "external organ (hand)" is striving to reveal the content, and aid in the evolution of the "inner organ (mind)" so the hands of the race have been revealing the needs, aspirations and achievements of humanity during the various stages of civilization. Man's development may be traced by the products of his handicraft all along the line of his evolution. His physical, mental and moral powers may be measured in any period by his courage, skill, and taste in grappling with his environment and making it over to satisfy his physical needs, and express his inner life. All discovery, inventions and progress in science and art are the direct product of the mind working through the hand.

The first plastic medium used by primitive man for

[1] Educational Problems, Hall, Chapter XX.
[2] Psychology of the Play Gifts, Snider.   Sigma Publishing Co.

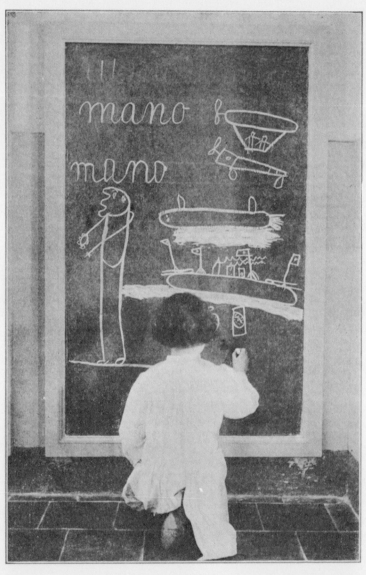

A Roman Patriot, Age Four, making a Picture Story of the
War with Turkey.

The soldier, torpedo boat, and warship are in evidence.

the concrete expression of thought was clay. By the use of this material, which responds to every light touch of the fingers, children play themselves through experiences which train the mind to think and the hand to express. With both hands working together, they cultivate unconsciously some appreciation of form, size and contour. Sight and touch aid each other in the process of representing form in its three dimensions and in preparing for the more abstract art of drawing. They are gaining in observation, motor control and inventiveness, while they gratify that impulse so strong in children, to attack and change all that will yield to their touch.[1]

"Whatever things are plastic to his hand, those things he must remodel into shapes of his own, and the result of the remodeling, however useless it may be, gives him more pleasure than the original thing. The mania of young children for breaking and pulling apart whatever is given them, is more often the expression of a rudimentary constructive impulse than of a destructive one."[2]

The child's first use of all materials seems capricious. He loves to play with them; to change and modify them. He often takes an object apart the moment it is completed. He wants results to follow quickly on the heels of effort. Later, interest in the result predominates, and the activity is merely the means of producing it. Improvement of technique is striven for in order that the product may fulfill the worker's standards of workmanship.

Ernest Beckwith Kent names the four stages that

[1] Modeling in the Primary School, Sargent.
[2] Principles of Psychology, James, Vol. II, p. 426. Henry Holt and Co.

L

the child passes through in the development of constructive motive, (1) instinctive, (2) imitational, (3) play-utility, (4) adult-utility.

The instinctive stage with the young child is one of pure manipulation when pleasure comes from being the cause of change. Every mother has seen children sift and pile sand, pat and roll clay, scribble with crayon and revel in the use of all materials that invite these responses.

"Along with this wholly sensational pleasure of pure manipulation there is probably the beginning of an intellectual pleasure, and from this side the activity might be called experimentation as well as manipulation — the child wants to see what will happen."[1]

Then follows the time when attempts are made to imitate the activities of grown-ups. Now in the course of instinctive activity, something with a resemblance to a familiar object or process catches the child's eye and he says, "Do you want to buy some sugar?" (sand); "I'm making pies" (clay, sand, mud); "Here's a man" (drawing). With this accidentally discovered clew to a possibility of the material, he now makes many objects or carries out processes familiar to him.

Kent refers to the "mud pie" as the most typical representation of the transition to the imitation stage.

"Here is clearly a double pleasure in manipulation and imitation. Heretofore he has been contented to 'heap and dig away,' his sand, but now he adds to the pleasure of modifying a plastic material, that of reproducing a household occupation. The pie is clearly not an end in itself. Building with blocks is perhaps

[1] The Constructive Interests of Children, Kent, p. 11. Teachers College, Columbia University.

the line of work that depends most exclusively upon the imitation motive — manipulation pleasure would seem small compared with that obtained from plastic materials, and the product is still nothing." [1]

The play product is typified by the making of clay dishes which serve day after day in housekeeping play, or by marbles that can be rolled. The adult-utility

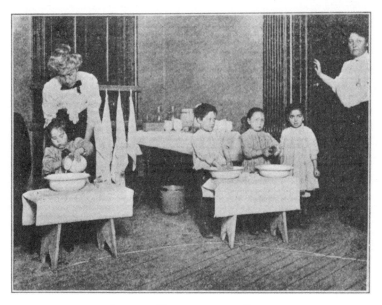

AFTER A PLAYTIME WITH CLAY.

one, by the making and firing of a vase or flowerpot that will serve the purpose of holding cut flowers or a plant.

These periods of growth cannot be measured entirely by years, nor does one cease absolutely as another comes.

[1] The Constructive Interests of Children, Kent, p. 12.

Recourse must be made to previous levels for new skills, new possibilities of materials, new ideas to be expressed. But there comes a time when play products cease to satisfy, and the child, entering the third stage in this development, craves more of real results for all his efforts. Thus he looks toward that fourth and final phase of man's work when process is almost lost sight of in the eagerness for product. The attitude in this stage should still be, and actually is, where working conditions are right, just as joyous as in previous stages.

Watching the activities of the children in a Montessori school, one is impressed with the belief that here the beginning stages of the constructive motive are well guarded and reverenced by thoughtful observers of child life. It is this fact which warrants this discussion, for Doctor Montessori brings no new contribution in connection with the use of clay as educative material. As far as the writer observed, the possibilities of clay had not been as fully developed in the Children's Houses as they have been in American kindergartens and primary schools.

The chapter dealing with clay is brief. The following quotations give some indication of its spirit and content:

"In consideration, however, of the system of liberty which I proposed, I did not like to make the children copy anything, and, in giving them clay to fashion in their own manner, I did not direct the children to produce useful things." [1]

"Many little ones model the objects which they have seen at home, especially kitchen furniture, water jugs, pots, and pans.

[1] The Montessori Method, p. 162.

Sometimes, we are shown a simple cradle containing a baby brother or sister. At first it is necessary to place written descriptions upon these objects, as it is necessary to do with the free design. Later on, however, the models are easily recognizable, and the children learn to reproduce the geometric solids." [1]

Doctor Montessori refers to "The School of Educative Art" where civic pride and artistic skill are acquired by the methods of Professor Randone, its founder. These have been adopted to some extent in the Children's Houses. For example, the vase form much used by Randone is accepted as a suitable form for modeling because of its "adaptability to every modification of form and its susceptibility to the most diverse ornamentation."

" After two or three lessons the little pupils are already enthusiastic about the construction of vases, and they preserve very carefully their own products, in which they take pride. With their plastic art they then model little objects, eggs or fruits, with which they themselves fill the vases. One of the first undertakings is the simple vase of red clay filled with eggs of white clay; then comes the modeling of the vase with one or more spouts, of the narrow-mouthed vase, of the vase with a handle, of that with two or three handles, of the tripod, of the amphora." [2]

" For children of the age of five or six, the work of the potter's wheel begins." [2]

She has also adapted from "The School of Educative Art" the idea of making bricks which are afterward fired and built by the children's hands into miniature walls.

"But what most delights the children is the work of building a wall with little bricks, and seeing a little house, the fruit of their

---

[1] The Montessori Method, p. 242.   [2] *Ibid.*, p. 166.

own hands, rise in the vicinity of the ground in which are growing plants, also cultivated by them. Thus the age of childhood epitomizes the principal primitive labors of humanity, when the human race, changing from the nomadic to the stable condition, demanded of the earth its fruit, built itself shelter, and devised vases to cook the foods yielded by the fertile earth." [1]

Doctor Montessori not only provides in her schools such suitable stimuli for constructive activity as clay and blocks — but she grants that other necessary condition for self-expression — personal liberty. Here the instinctive and imitative periods are permitted to have their full measure of time. A child may pile up and tear down his blocks or other materials (with the exception of didactic apparatus) indefinitely without interruption. Playing with all things that attract him in his environment, he gets from them what he may. As the quality of what he has learned to do by himself no longer satisfies him because his ideas of form and color are now more accurate and clear, and his ideals of workmanship are higher, he is eager for guidance, for definite instruction from an older person, possibly for the use of tools that supplement the work of his hands. It is on some such basis as this that the potter's wheel would have a place in the child's work in clay. To the teacher belongs the task of determining when the help of direction or implement is sufficiently felt as a need by the child to warrant its presentation. There are those who would question that the child would feel the need of the potter's wheel or that he would possess, at five or six years, the capacity for the coördi-

[1] The Montessori Method, p. 166.

nation necessary to its use. Doctor Montessori's reply
to this criticism of the use of the wheel would probably
be that there are some things which must be brought to
the child earlier than he manifests the need for them,
to the end that he may at a later time be freer because
he is in control of the mechanisms for expression of ideas
or construction of objects in manual labor.

Probably the same question will be raised by most
people when typewriters are advocated for the earlier
grades. People are slow to move away from old ideas
and habits. "Because typewriters have always been
used by people of high school age and above, therefore
they cannot be used by young children," is their type
of thought. Experiments like that tried with Winifred
Stoner and other precocious children who began at three
or four to play with the typewriter and who at seven
or eight could write letters upon it, are either disbelieved
or ridiculed by the average parent or teacher. Thus in
all times have innovations been treated by the many.
Only the few have been willing to test out by further
experimentation the merit of the suggested new departure.

With the general principles that make it possible for
each child to do the thing he wishes to do in the way
that he wishes to do it, and that make the directress,
in the spirit of the scientist, value each period of development, caring less for immediate products and more
for growth in a broad sense, results may be attainable
in the education of children that up to the present few
people have dared to dream of and to experiment for.
When a normal child's personality is set free, when he is
encouraged to enjoy his environment without restraints

THE GARDENERS.

"The possessors of the earth . . . are sowing or hoeing, watering or examining, the surface of the soil, watching for the sprouting of plants." — *Montessori.*

save those imposed by good breeding, the rights of others and respect for property, he is sure to grow by leaps and bounds, providing that the environment is wholesome. This condition Doctor Montessori has striven to provide. Her equipment does not contain all things ideal, nor do her plans include all the desirable features of the best American schools. What she claims and what she really seems to be accomplishing is in a measure stated in the following paragraphs:

"The children work by themselves, and, in doing so, make a conquest of active discipline and independence in all the acts of daily life, just as through daily conquests they progress in intellectual development. Directed by an intelligent teacher, who watches over their physical development as well as over their intellectual and moral progress, children are able with our methods to arrive at a splendid physical development, and, in addition to this, there unfolds within them, in all its perfection, the soul, which distinguishes the human being." [1]

"In our efforts with the child, external acts are the means which stimulate internal development, and they again appear as its manifestation, the two elements being inextricably intertwined. Work develops the child spiritually; but the child with a fuller spiritual development works better, and his improved work delights him, — hence he continues to develop spiritually." [2]

Some students of the Montessori method have questioned her statement that clay "serves for the study of the psychic individuality of the child in his spontaneous manifestations, but not for his education." If one reads the chapter on "Manual Labor" and the discussion of free plastic work in the chapter on "Intellectual Education," it will be plainly seen that Doctor Montessori

[1] The Montessori Method, p. 375.   [2] *Ibid.*, p. 353.

gives clay its place as a valuable stimulus in the self-
making process of the child. All handwork, all expression, reveals the child not only to his teacher but to
himself. Upon this revelation the teacher bases the
next conditioning of the child in order that he may be
stimulated to different and higher tasks; the child
finding the limits of his present powers of seeing, knowing and executing, looks more closely and tries again:
the result is a more fully expressed idea and a finer technique of performance.

It is a great thing for a teacher to be able to study
a child until she knows its needs, its temperament,
stage of development, social environment and physical
strength; for her to place then within its reach such
stimuli as shall meet these conditions; and with sympathy, patience and the simplest and best technique of
instruction to permit the child to carry on a process of
self-education. Under such conditions, we can scarcely
overestimate the value of clay as a stimulus.

1. It serves
   a. The child, as a means of self-expression revealing him to himself.
   b. The teacher, as a means of studying the child.
2. It gratifies the natural impulse to investigate and
   change materials.
3. Results are obtained quickly, so that fleeting interests are expressed.
4. Clear mental images are developed, the child
   seeing in his lump of clay the possibility of
   a finished product.
5. Natural forms are presented before type forms.

6. Perception of the third dimensions is a preparation for drawing.
7. The tactible, visual and motor memories are all brought into activity.
8. Perception of form, size and contour is encouraged.
9. Skill of hand and enjoyment of creative effort result.
10. Accuracy, observation, concentration, patience and perseverance are stimulated.

Turning to another subject, drawing, one finds the value of preparation for another activity and the educative value of self-expression embodied in Doctor Montessori's theory and practice. Through the exercises in design the child learns to write before writing. There is also something to be said in favor of such exercises in connection with their relation to drawing, as by means of these designs the child's passion for scribbling is directed into right channels. He is unconsciously mastering the art of holding and guiding the medium of drawing — whether it be chalk, marking pencil or charcoal — and the resulting muscular control and judgment in proportion, color discrimination and arrangement aid in making drawing an easier mode of expression.

Every child revels in the joys of picture making long before he goes to school. His crude drawings represent ideas rather than objects as they really appear. "Young children draw what they know about objects rather than what their eyes see at any given moment." [1] It took the human race a long time to discover the principles of perspective and of light and shade. A study of the

[1] Fine and Industrial Arts in Elementary Schools, Sargent.

Madonnas will reveal the gradual and comparatively recent appreciation of what is seen and of how to express it. The child must be given full opportunity to use his own symbols.

The time will come when he realizes that his drawing does not represent the object as he sees it. The resulting dissatisfaction gives occasion for suggestions involving principles of perspective and light and shade. These will make it possible for him to criticise his own work and to give better expression to his thought. This time does not usually arrive before the sixth year. There are suggestions of it appearing in first grades, however, as the following will illustrate. The children's first pose work had been that of a classmate standing before the class. The problem was to tell with paints that a girl with . . . . dress, ... ribbons and . . . . hair stood with her back to the class. On another day, the model was seated on a chair. It happened that her skirt fell over the side of the chair toward the class. Out of a class of twenty, nineteen showed the framework of the chair through the dress; the twentieth child did not. Her picture, when placed with others upon the bulletin board, became the point of departure to a discussion of telling what is *seen* rather than what is *actually present*.

So some child, too, hits upon the fact that a small tree, or house, or person, placed higher up on his paper looks like a tree, or a house, or a person in the distance. Out of this grows the principle that things near at hand look larger than things of the same size far away. The teacher must know what constitutes acceptable early drawings. She must recognize the arrival of the time when the child is finding his way to the higher level and must be ready to appreciate and guide his work gradually toward correct representation of what he as an individual sees from his particular point of observation. The gradual mastery of these principles underlies the courses of study in drawing for the grades before the high school. The child should not be hurried into them by copying the perspective drawings of older people.

The mechanical skill acquired from the exercises in design in the use of metal insets, makes it easy for the child to draw quite accurately a straight, slanting or curved line, or to sweep his brush across the paper with freedom and definite purpose. Doctor Montessori also permits much "free" drawing, hence there is the possibility of reënforcement of each kind by the other.

Most American teachers of art, swinging away from the copying tendency, insist that drawing for little children (to be educational) must be entirely free hand; that in mass work there shall be no outline to limit the pencil stroke. Some, however, advise outlines for teaching color effects and for beginning ideas in proportion and balance, believing that without bounds or limitations the child can at first produce only confused blotches, mental images being too hazy for definite expression. Doctor Montessori allows children to fill in with pencil or brush outlines of birds, flowers, butterflies and trees, as well as conventional borders. This not only trains in mechanical skill, but stimulates study of color that is true to life. Th child observes colors in these natural objects and then reproduces them from memory.

"The fact that the child must remember the color of the objects represented in the design encourages him to observe those things which are about him.   And then, too, he wishes to be able to fill

in more difficult designs. Only those children who know how to keep the color within the outline and to re- produce the right colors may proceed to the more ambi- tious work. These designs are very easy, and often very effective, sometimes display- ing real artistic work." [1]

COLORING FROM OUTLINE.

Such work is balanced by drawing in which chil- dren express their own conceptions of form and their individual power to indicate the same. This prevents their be- coming dependent upon outlines.   According to Doctor Montessori, their design work does for the color sense what free-hand drawing does for form.   The child has a passion for color, its appeal being stronger than that of form.   Just as, regardless of perspective, he draws striking objects, making them stand out larger and quite out of proportion to other (to him) less im- portant ones, so the bit of brilliant color appeals to him and is given first place in his picture.

Gathering up these points with reference to drawing,

[1] The Montessori Method, p. 244.

we have the following ideas for our consideration and discussion :

1. Place development before result.

2. Preserve children's work as a record of growth.

3. Make use of sense training as a means of delineating form. Sight alone cannot tell of form, there must also be touch.

4. Less instructions and more free childish imaginative sweep should be given during the precious time of dreams and fancies.

5. A child would rather draw his own mental images than another's.

6. Since the child would rather draw what he knows about an object than what he sees of it at any one time, he should be allowed to do so, but when he begins to question or to manifest dissatisfaction with his own power to tell what he sees, attention should be called to appearance rather than facts.

7. Mediums are most desirable which call into play the larger muscles of the hand and arm; thus strain and tension are avoided.

8. Long-continued application does no harm if interest and enjoyment in the work is keen, but the moment real interest ceases, drudgery is the result.

9. A child may look and not see. Scientific observation of children helps us to know their needs.

10. There is a delightful confidence and joy in just drawing when imagination supplies deficiencies. Do not destroy this by insistence upon mechanical accuracy.

11. The child likes strong contrasts at first. Do not force refined color upon him.

12. Drawing should connect itself with life, and its influence should gradually aid in the development of self-control, concentration, appreciation of beauty, independence, and a critical attitude.

13. The unconscious imitation of other children and adults is necessary for a child's development, but where that imitation becomes conscious it tends to weaken rather than strengthen the personality.

14. All designs should lead to good arrangement and ideas of rhythm in color and form.

Like American educators, Doctor Montessori does not believe in relying solely upon the child's own art production for the development of his æsthetic nature. She would therefore surround the school child with the best that nature and art can provide. Her plans for her Children's Houses were carefully worked out along this ideal because she believes strongly in the influence of environment, especially upon the little child, when powers of resistance are limited.

"The environment acts more strongly upon the individual life the less fixed and strong this individual life may be." [1]

That art has another mission to perform besides that of cultivating a taste for the beautiful in color, line, composition and form is shown in another quotation:

"Above the blackboards are hung attractive pictures, chosen carefully, representing simple scenes in which children would naturally be interested. Among the pictures in our 'Children's Houses' in Rome we have hung a copy of Raphael's 'Madonna della Seggiola,' and this picture we have chosen as the emblem

[1] The Montessori Method, p. 105.

of the 'Children's Houses.'   For indeed, these 'Children's Houses' represent not only social progress, but universal human progress, and are closely related to the elevation of the idea of motherhood, to the progress of woman and to the protection of her offspring. In this beautiful conception, Raphael has not only shown us the Madonna as a Divine Mother holding in her arms the babe who is greater than she, but by the side of this symbol of all motherhood, he has placed the figure of St. John, who represents humanity. So in Raphael's picture we see humanity rendering homage to maternity, — maternity, the sublime fact in the definite triumph of humanity.   In addition to this beautiful symbolism, the picture has a value as being one of the greatest works of art of Italy's greatest artist." [1]

A great picture, like a great building, or statue, or like great music, may and does give refined satisfying pleasure through the senses, but it must go a step further and interpret life — life that is nature's and life that is man's. [2]

[1] The Montessori Method, p. 82.
[2] The Principles of Art Education, Münsterberg, pp. 112–113.

M

CHAPTER VIII

WE are indebted to no less a man than John Fiske for an essay on "The Meaning of Infancy." In it are reviewed the facts of the parallelisms between the longer periods of babyhood and the higher places in the scale of animal life. The simpler forms of animals come into the world so fully developed that they manage for themselves from the beginning. The more complex forms, such as nestling, puppy, kitten and lamb, experience a period of helplessness before becoming independent creatures of their kind. With amœba, jellyfish, snail, turtle, larvæ and the like, there is no parental responsibility, for the relationship of the adult to the young is severed at the time of depositing the eggs or of giving birth to the new generation. These young creatures are smaller than they will become; a function or two may develop as maturity approaches, but the equipment for self-preservation through warding off enemies, and through securing the necessities for existence is practically in complete working order at birth.

The essence of babyhood, then, is not merely smallness of structure, but that incompleteness of functioning which demands from an adult the care that preserves life. In the mammalia, this care takes the form of feeding the young from the body of the mother, of sheltering it from weather and attack, of stimulating it into activity that works toward independent action.

This condition of dependence upon the adult is by far greatest in human beings, reaching its culmination among civilized people where the young are theoretically (and often actually) not independent until a college course has been completed, though the maladjustments of the social and economic order do force many children out into the realm of self-maintenance before they can be considered physically, mentally or morally matured.

Infancy has had its part in creating and developing the home. In the long ago the mother had to stay with her babe. In time, the father stayed too, in order to protect the child and mother. The helplessness of the infant, the association in ministering to it, awoke affection. And thus the foundations of family life and of morality were laid.

In time, through organization, the demands upon men were lessened. They saved time and energy by combining against common enemies, by capturing or eradicating them. The leisure gained from hunting and fighting was spent about the home. Gradually tasks which the mother had worked at exclusively became the father's, and her labor became more and more confined to the limits of a small outdoor space, finally within the limits of "four walls and a ceiling." A German emperor is credited with the statement that a woman's interest should be confined to the "Three K's," which translated into English constitute the "Three C's,"—children, church and cooking.

There is a familiar sound to the expression, "Woman's

place is the home." And how true it is, if we bear in mind that the home is subject to the same law of growth to which every institution, to which every plant and animal, to which the world itself has been and is subject. Out of *no* house in a far, far distant time came *a* house; out of that staying together in almost anything which nature provided in the form of a cave, came crude hand-made dwellings; and out of these, came finally our modern homes of simple or more pretentious convenience and beauty.

A similar transformation has gone on within the house, not only with reference to material things, but also with reference to the intangible things — relationships between husband and wife, parents and children, sisters and brothers, host and guest. It is the evolutionary nature of the house and the home which most people ignore when they reiterate that "Woman's place is the home," and give to it the limits already suggested.

It verges on the trite to say that woman is, more and more, going out into the world's activities. She finds her work in the shop where clothes are made, bread is baked, fruits, vegetables and meats are canned. She finds it in the dairy where milk is bottled and butter and cheese are made, in the cold storage houses where the food stuffs are held, and in stores where the necessities for the life of her family are being sold. She finds it in care given to the source of the water supply, the disposal of garbage, the cleansing of streets, the consideration of health ordinances. She finds it in the church and schoolhouse where her children are taught, in the moving picture show and in the dance hall, where her children are entertained (though not always for their welfare). She finds it in the council, in the board of education, and, in some states, in the legislature. Woman's sphere is the home, but the home of to-day has had its walls expanded by a new order of industrial and commercial life almost to the uttermost boundaries of the earth. These newer and bigger responsibilities of the home call for strong, enlightened women, women equal to bear the growing pains involved in thinking, and the struggle involved in adjustment.[1]

"The house, thus considered, tends to assume in its evolution a significance more exalted than even the English word "home" expresses. It does not consist of walls alone, though these walls be the pure and shining guardians of that intimacy which is the sacred symbol of the family. The home shall become more than this. It lives! It has a soul. It may be said to embrace its inmates with the tender, consoling arms of woman. It is the giver of moral life, of blessings; it cares for, it educates and feeds, the little ones. Within it, the tired workman shall find rest and newness of life. He shall find there the intimate life of the family, and its happiness.

" The new woman, like the butterfly come forth from the chrysalis, shall be liberated from all those attributes which once made her desirable to man only as the source of the material blessings of existence. She shall be, like man, an individual, a free human being, a social worker; and, like man, she shall seek blessing and repose within the house, the house which has been reformed and communized." [2]

No old order is ever restored, hence we must face some questions rising out of the new. Several states have recently declared by the passage of "Mother's Pension

[1] Newer Ideals of Peace, Addams, Chapters VI, VII.
[2] The Montessori Method, pp. 68–69.

FILLING WATERING POTS AT THE FOUNTAIN IN THE PINCIAN GARDENS.
The flowers need a bath.

Laws" that the value of the woman as a mother in her home is greater to her children and to the state eventually, than is her value as a laundress, a seamstress, or clerk, by means of which she earns the price of food, clothing and shelter to keep her family physically alive.

Other ways of meeting the necessity of the mother's entire support of the family have resulted in the day nursery, the infant school, the kindergarten, the settlement and, most recently, the Children's House. Of this Doctor Montessori says:

"We can no longer say that the convenience of leaving her children takes away from the mother a natural social duty of first importance; namely, that of caring for and educating her tender offspring. No, for to-day the social and economic evolution calls the working woman to take her place among wage earners, and takes away from her by force those duties which would be most dear to her! The mother must, in any event, leave her child, and often with the pain of knowing him to be abandoned. The advantages furnished by such institutions are not limited to the laboring classes, but extend also to the general middle-class, many of whom work with the brain. Teachers, professors, often obliged to give private lessons after school hours, frequently leave their children to the care of some rough and ignorant maid-of-all-work. Indeed, the first announcement of the 'Children's House' was followed by a deluge of letters from persons of the better class demanding that these helpful reforms be extended to their dwellings." [1]

The present outlook would indicate that society will do much during this generation to promote both the home and these outside agencies. Society now main-

[1] The Montessori Method, p. 66.

tains that the home must not only be kept intact, but must be improved by requiring of prospective home-makers definite physical, intellectual and social quali-fications. Marriage laws are gradually attacking the problem. Courses in domestic economy and other subjects are indirectly helping in its solution. Plans for continuation schools that shall educate for mother-hood and fatherhood are being discussed.

All this points to the time when it will be counted a disgrace that many children die annually of preventable causes because of the ignorance of individuals and com-munities; that so many who live cannot measure up to the standards of the Baby Health Contests. It will also be counted a disgrace that dispositions are em-bittered, that there are established habits of thought and feeling which are selfish, morbid, and in other ways antisocial and immoral. It will be counted quite as much a disgrace that children grow up never knowing and never fulfilling the possibilities of the alertness, the richness, the service that their individual mental endowments make possible but that educational efforts pass over.[1]

Old as are the relationships of parents to child, in the matters of physical preservation, of intellectual super-vision and moral guidance, some are slow to recognize the importance of conscious, intelligent child study. It is as though the vast majority of people confuse the facts of once having been children, of seeing many children, and of being the physical parents of children with the knowledge that grows out of special preparation

[1] The Education of the Child, Key.   The Boy Problem, Forbush.

A CORNER OF THE MUSIC ROOM OF THE PINCIAN HILL SCHOOL.

Children are given cut-steel rests, notes and bars, and a staff ruled on coarse paper. From this they build up their musical phrases.

for that most difficult of difficult tasks — the rearing of children.[1]

There are many kinds of homes. They can all be grouped within the possible combinations expressed and implied below.

1. Meager in material environment,
   - a. and also in intellectual and social life.
   - b. but comfortable in intellectual and social life.
   - c. but rich in intellectual and social life.

2. Comfortable in material environment,
   - a. but poor in intellectual and social advantages.
   - b. and well-to-do in intellectual and social advantages.
   - c. and rich in intellectual and social advantages.

3. Wealthy in material environment,
   - a. but poor in intellectual and social stimuli.
   - b. and well-to-do in intellectual and social stimuli.
   - c. and rich in intellectual and social stimuli.

Every one can think of cases from real life or from life portrayed in books or on the stage, that illustrate these types.

(1. a.) The child that is brought to court and placed under the jurisdiction of others besides his parents because the parents have shown themselves unable or incapable of caring for him properly.

[1] The School in the Home, Berle.

(1. *b*, *c*.) Many a boy who has attained eminence came from this kind of home.

(2. *b*.) Probably most of the people who read this come from homes of this type.

(2. *c*.) The so-called precocious children [1] are frequently found in such homes.

(3. *a*.) "The Poor Little Rich Girl" had a father who was busy and successful making money; a mother absorbed with society; a maid and governess, who likewise were busy with affairs of their own; and a corps of special teachers for dancing, music, French, etc., whose interests were in the remuneration received for efforts supposedly made. Only the physician who was with her at birth knew when he met her again on her eighth birthday how she had been starved.

(3. *c*.) "The Second Generation" portrays the father who has the intelligence to see, and the courage to prevent his material wealth from causing the degeneracy of his son and daughter.

One could refer to those whose names are household words because of the fine activities associated with them. Unfortunately, the daily press brings also the names which stand for the worst types under this grouping.

While Doctor Montessori's book is being principally considered in relation to school ideals and methods, one who reads her Inaugural Address and her chapter on " Discipline " [2] is prone to wonder if her greater service is not after all rendered to parents in helping them to view child life as a whole — to see from what it should

[1] Precocious Children.   Pedagogical Seminary, December, 1912.
[2] The Montessori Method, Chapters III, V.

spring and how it should be conditioned in order that its contribution to the human race may be a positive one. Thoughtfully reading this book one will see that the days of preparation for the advent of a new member of the family should not be confined to the making of an elaborate layette; some time should be given to knowing what a young baby's physical needs will be, what desirable habits can and should be fostered early, what intellectual hungers will first be manifested, and how all of these may be met for the health and happiness of the child. And as the weeks pass into months and the months into years, there should be the continuance of thoughtful preparation that will insure bodily, mental and social well-being.

Hygienic and sanitary surroundings, a simple wholesome diet, plenty of sleep at regular hours, abundance of fresh air at night, out-of-door activities by day, all have their part to play in making the child physically sound. It probably takes some courage to withhold unwholesome sweets and always keep to suitable foods when one's hostess sets the dainty and the rich before the child.

Parents who do not allow children's naps to be disturbed for anything short of emergency, who protect them from teasing play that brings on a tearful condition, who safeguard them from the contagion of common towels, handkerchiefs and eating utensils, may sometimes be considered over-fastidious, but the resulting health and happiness prove the wisdom of such a policy. Simple hygienic rules and corresponding habits are easily established, such as the following:

Always wash your hands before touching food.

THE HAND-WASHING ACTIVITY.

A physician has recently said: "The greatest, and most prevalent crime of our day is the dirty hand."

Always throw away pieces of food that have dropped on the floor.

Always use a very clean part of your handkerchief to wipe your eyes.

A well-known student of children has made the assertion that practically all the correct physical habits should be established before the age of six. Of course, the nature of habit formation must be understood and the parent must definitely decide the order of acquirement.[1]

Since the child's self-education begins soon after his arrival and is fostered by the things which come to him as he is bathed and dressed and fed and taken out, as well as by the toys that fond relatives and friends shower upon him, it is unnecessary to answer the question so often asked by earnest parents, "When should a child's education begin?"[2]

When the rattle stage and the putting everything into his mouth have become a part of the child's past, when walking and some control of oral speech have been acquired, didactic material may be put within his reach. If he finds on the shelf with familiar playthings the broad stair, the sandpaper board, and the hearing boxes (see pp. 69, 76), the day will come when he will take one or the other down for use. A lesson may be given immediately; it may be that of building up the blocks and then taking them down while the child watches. Left with the material, the child will probably attempt a similar performance. His efforts will at first be full of

[1] Education, Thorndike, Chapter VI. Talks to Teachers, James, Chapter VIII.
[2] Mental Growth and Control, Oppenheim, Chapter VII.

errors, but so long as he is attempting to place blocks upon blocks, he may remain at the activity.   When his efforts show some discrimination of size, there should come the formal lesson making this explicit.   The mother

ITALIAN CHILDREN ENJOYING THE MERRY TRADITIONAL GAME OF "ROUND AND ROUND THE VILLAGE."

will take the smallest and the largest blocks and carry out the three Seguin steps.   Left to himself, the child will redouble his efforts at piling, making somewhat closer discriminations.   Again the mother will give a lesson, and another until the ideas of small, smaller, smallest;

and large, larger, largest, seem to be grasped. The final stage is reached when without error and hesitation the child makes and remakes the tower. With these possibilities exhausted, or possibly before, he has turned to some other material which has been similarly treated.

If the parent is interested in seeing how much of the skill developed with one piece of apparatus will be transferred to another, the frame of cylindrical insets differing in thickness and length may next be offered to the child. The adjectives that apply here are again large, larger, largest; small, smaller, smallest. The presentation should in such a case be confined to taking the insets out and putting them back without any comment as to difference in size of holes and corresponding cylinders. Evidence of the transfer should be looked for in the child's spontaneous scrutiny of the objects rather than the mere promiscuous trying one and then another until the proper places are found. If a careful record has been kept of the number of times the child played with the tower, of the number of trials made in each play period with it, and of the exact number of minutes consumed, and a similar record is made of his use of this set of cylindrical insets, there will be some basis for consideration of the question as to the extent to which power is transferred. To secure still more exact data in the above experiment, the cylindrical insets should have been used in an initial test; the amount of time, the number of efforts, the character of this (hit and miss or thoughtful scrutiny), and the degree of success at the close of the period, should have been recorded. The tower should then be given for the practice of the power of discriminating size. When this has reached its highest level of success, the cylindrical insets should again be given. The effort at this time would constitute the final test; the data of time trials, errors (due to not scrutinizing and to mistaken judgments), and successes (due to accident and to judgment), could then be used in comparison with the same data on the initial test and the transfer of power be reckoned. A number of such studies have been made upon adults in psychological laboratories. These would be helpful to any one desiring to know the method of procedure that results in accurate scientific data. By the average parent this exact measuring will not be desired, as it makes greater demands upon time and energy than can be given. But some recording of observations should be made if parents are to acquire definite information regarding the value of these materials in child development.

It so happened that at a demonstration of Montessori materials to adults this summer, one of these less carefully conducted experiments was made. A girl of three was given the cylindrical insets differing in thickness. She watched while the instructor took them out and put them in. She was given a chance to do likewise. When it was evident that she understood that the process was one of "putting in," the next step was taken. The teacher said, "This is thin, this is thick," and put each into its respective place, filled in the other openings and then took them all out, saying again, "This is thin, this is thick," for the two extremes. The child's next effort involved the spontaneous saying of these words and a slight attempt at being guided by the difference. As

N

time went on she manifested quicker appreciation of exact and of inexact fittings, and then of judging carefully before making an attempt at fitting. The extremes were more easily done. Though her interest was still strong, her attention was distracted purposely to other objects. Later she was allowed to come back to the same frame of insets; and still later to the frame in which the cylinders varied both in height and thickness. A general account was kept of the time and tendency to use judgment, rather than of the trial and error method. The resetting was accomplished more quickly, with fewer errors and with more thoughtfulness. Just how much improvement there was in speed and accuracy could not be determined because the experiment was not carefully conditioned.

Other points for observation should also be sought by those who have the opportunity of seeing children with these materials. Among them are the age at which such activities as the putting in and taking out the cylindrical insets, the building of the tower and the broad and long stairs, the matching of the color bobbins, the setting of the sound boxes in order, counting, etc., make their strongest and most persisting appeals. This would undoubtedly mean placing many materials within the child's reach, being ready to give the appropriate lesson for any piece chosen at a given time and then making a record of how long the child stayed with it, how often he went back to it, and when he ceased to pay any further attention to it.

There should be noted, too, evidences of the child's application of the ideas or skill gained to other things

A SWING IS AN OLD AND FAVORITE PIECE OF PLAY APPARATUS.

Between the stage of the first timorous holding of one's self in place and the final fearless easy swinging as high as one can go lies exhilarating, healthful activity.

in his environment. Does he think these in terms of large, larger and largest; small, smaller, smallest? Of long, longer, longest; short, shorter, shortest? Does he think flowers and ribbons in terms of light, lighter, lightest; dark, darker, darkest? Differences in size, color, texture, temperature, weight and form are everywhere about him. Is he more sensitive to them because of the experience with materials which artificially embody these qualities apart from the natural home and outdoor environment? Is such sensitiveness an added source of control over pleasure in that natural environment?

To the parents familiar with kindergarten material, another feature of interest will be the relative degree of appeal (and the age at which it is made) of the gifts. An ideal equipment for the home would therefore be comprised of both the didactic materials and the gifts and occupation (in enlarged form). The arrangement at the Children's Class of the summer session at the University of Montana is suggestive here. On two low shelves on one side of the large playroom were placed the Montessori materials; on similar shelves on the opposite side were placed the kindergarten materials. For a portion of each day, the children were at liberty to choose from either kind of material. The instructors responded to requests for suggestions, showed how the didactic materials were to be used, and kept a general record of what occurred. A specific one was out of the question, since two people could not possibly keep tab on twenty active children playing with many more than twenty playthings. Since there was only a single set of gifts, group work with the same was not possible.

WATCHING THE MOTHER BIRD FEED HER YOUNG.
(University of Montana.)

It was attempted with the so-called occupation materials, such as clay, crayons, paper and scissors. This class suggests the other ideal feature for the home experiment, — the presence of other children, though not necessarily so many; for the essentially social capacity of the child must not be ignored.

"The third quality that must strike the scientific observer of little children is their remarkable desire for, and facility in, social intercourse. Even in extreme infancy, the baby longs to have some one near him. In his first days he prefers to lie in a lap rather than in a cushioned crib. Only with protestations and cries will he break his social bonds and voyage off into the lonely land of sleep. In the first year he greets animals and babies as his peers. After his first year, any child who seeks solitude is something of a monster. This intelligent interpretation of, and response to, the social forces about him early mark the child as the master of all living things. At three years old, he reads a face as adults read books. At six he has passed through and at least partially assimilated most of the social experiences of life." [1]

The following questions have been suggested by the writer's discussions of Montessori and kindergarten principles with mothers:

1. What is the fallacy of the argument, "But I don't want my child to go to the Children's House or the kindergarten. He is the only baby I have and he will grow up so soon"? Or, "I want my child to dig in the dirt until he is six or seven. It will then be time enough for him to begin to learn"?

2. What injustice has been done to the child who has been trained to no feeling of responsibility for doing things that help in the daily tasks of the house or yard,

[1] National Education Association, Barnes, 1908.

who has arrived at the age of six without the ability to dress and undress himself, to hang up and take down his own belongings? What disappointment is likely to meet the parent who says, "My child is not to work now. I want him to play and have a good time and when he is older he will help me"? What distinction should be made between play, work and drudgery?

3. Why is the policy of paying the child with money or gifts for things that he must do an expensive one? Why should a child derive money from two sources: (a) a small allowance, and (b) earning through doing regularly a necessary task as soon as he knows what money is for? What are the pernicious elements from the standpoint of the child's welfare as well as from the standpoint of family economy, of giving out pennies, nickels, etc., for use at the candy shops and picture shows?

4. How much foundation is there in the statement of G. Stanley Hall, that "the child's emotional attitudes, his moods and disposition are in a measure determined by the time he reaches his third birthday"? What suggestion does this carry to persons who enjoy teasing or seeing children teased to the point of an outburst of tears of angry retaliation or of prolonged pouting? What suggestion does it carry to the person who says, "I know my boy doesn't obey me now, but when he is six, I'll turn him over to his father and he will straighten him out"?

5. Show that a lie is only a tool which an unorganized mind can seize to make its way out of a difficulty. Is it a natural consequence of a lie when the child refuses

to stay with the policeman while the mother at the railway station goes to the window to get her ticket validated, she having said to the runaway child some minutes before, "Come here or the policeman will get you"? Are such threats confined to any particular class of parents as measured by their financial, occupational or social position? What is the characteristic of the type? What remedy can you suggest for it?

6. What would happen if every parent understood the theory (and applied it) embodied in Aristotle's contention that three things only are necessary in the rearing of children successfully?

1st. Noble birth. (Not "blue blood" in the veins of parents, but "blue" conduct, conversation and thoughts in their daily intercourse with each other and children.) [1]

2d. Habituation. (Training the child's conduct and conversation and thought in the direction of the fine examples which surround him.) [2]

3d. Rationalization. (Leading the child to understand the reasons for courtesy, honorableness, chastity and other virtues, individual and social, when he is ready to understand the reasons.) [3]

Show that Aristotle counted upon (a) the power of unconscious absorption, (b) conscious imitation of good copy and (c) ideas, to develop excellent characters.

Show to what extent Doctor Montessori seems to provide for a, b and c in her system.

[1] The Montessori Method, p. 69. [2] *Ibid.*, pp. 105–106.
[3] *Ibid.*, Chapter XXI.

CHAPTER IX

OTHER AGENCIES OF EARLY EDUCATION. THE KINDER-
GARTEN AND THE PRIMARY SCHOOL

THE home as an institution having opportunities and
responsibilities for the direct and systematic education
of children has been discussed. The agencies outside
the home doing similar work have come into existence
through the distribution and specialization of labor.
This historic fact is embodied in our very language.
The origin of the word "teacher" can be traced to a
word meaning "one who stands in the place of a parent."

The primary school is older than the kindergarten.
Like the kindergarten, it is newer than the grammar and
high school, the college and university. Not until the
basis for universal education was understood from the
standpoint of the welfare of the state and the individual,
were public funds levied upon to establish primary
schools.

This public support was followed by laws making
education compulsory. The Renaissance and the Ref-
ormation pointed the way to the worth of every human
being and his right as such to opportunities for development. The logical sequel to this was the establishment
of public school systems. Germany's system was the
first of the modern type. Its beginnings are to be found
in the work of Luther and Melanchthon from 1524 on.
The compulsory feature first made its appearance in

FREE PLAY IN THE KINDERGARTEN.

(Iowa State Teachers College.)

Weimar in 1619. The distinctive contention that an education, at least of an elementary character, must be the possession of every person if "national prosperity and stability" were to be attained, was most clearly seen in the beginning by Frederick the Great of Prussia.[1] His laws concerning education were formulated in 1763.

It took a long time for the idea of "for the masses as well as the upper classes" to permeate the machinery of political and religious institutions abroad and in the United States. In the meantime, philanthropic individuals and organizations came to the rescue by financing "Infant Schools" for the children of the less well-to-do. The wealthier people readily took care of their own children.

The use of public funds was made first in connection with the education of older pupils. Gradually it was drawn upon for younger and younger ones. As late as the second quarter of the nineteenth century, Boston still insisted that the rudiments of the Three R's should be a prerequisite for entrance into the public school system. These "beginnings" were sometimes acquired in the home, and sometimes in the "Dame Schools" supported by tuition. Some states show the influence of this early tendency to go from the top downward in matters of education and still hold to six as the school age entrance. This accounts in part for the slower development of the kindergarten in some states than in others.[2]

That some sensitive nerves connect with private and

[1] Text-Book on the History of Education, Monroe.
[2] The Kindergarten in American Education, Vanderwalker, p. 187.

public purses is evidenced when funds are requested for the expert training of young children. Men seem more willing to appropriate money for higher education and for business than for training during the important educative period of early childhood. This is natural and not to be condemned. The work of men has concerned itself chiefly with the production, transformation and distribution of the necessities and luxuries of life; they have had less responsibility than women for knowing the needs and capacities of *young* children. Those who have sought such insight have often been co-workers with women in movements looking to as favorable and full a consideration of children as of clams, or young colts, or cotton, or corn.

The children's era is approaching. Its arrival has been hastened through the comparative emancipation of woman from a subjection that was marital, intellectual, economical and political. Woman's influence is now being felt more and more, both indirectly in frank, helpful discussion with men and other women, and directly in expressing her best convictions for and against measures involving the physical, social and mental welfare of her own and her neighbor's children.

Considering the kindergarten and the primary school as we find them to-day, this must be said of them, as it may be said of the home, the church, the government or any other institution, — there are some very *poor*, some *mediocre*, some fairly *good* and some *excellent* ones. To judge any institution, or nation, for that matter, by its most defective members is, of course, folly. Since the "best" so far attained is illuminating in that it points to the path that must be taken to a better "best," the discussion of the modern American primary school and kindergarten will be limited, as in the case of the discussion of the Children's Houses, to facts concerning the higher types, not to travesties upon such schools, or yet to antique survivals of a darker pedagogical age. The writer has seen Children's Houses in Rome which Doctor Montessori could not and would not acknowledge as embodiments of her principles; she has seen kindergartens and primary schools in this country that fall far below the standards of both the founders and the advocates of these agencies. When scientific studies are made and their status plotted, it will probably be found that they follow what the experimental psychologist calls the normal curve. One sixth of them will fall into the *lowest or bad* group; another sixth into the *highest or excellent* group; and in between will be found

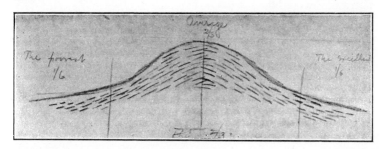

the other two thirds gathered most thickly about the *average or mediocre* group.

A study of one hundred kindergartens or primary schools that were representative of all existing types would tend to show the grouping suggested by the above diagram. Some of the criticisms of the kindergarten that have been made by advocates of the Montessori method would seem to be based on the *lower one sixth* group, for they ignore everything above that group. Whether it was a kindergarten of this type which was involved in the following incident, the writer does not know, but this kind of unscientific criticism is sometimes made by men and women who have influence in their communities; hence its pernicious effects. A mayor of a thriving city once stated in a meeting, "Now, gentlemen, I do not want to undermine what the lady has just said, but I want you to know my experience with the kindergarten. My children have been ruined by it; ruined physically, mentally and morally." The "lady" referred to had just called the attention of the convention assembled to the fact that the proposed measure before the state legislature raising the school age from four to six years would put the kindergarten upon the philanthropic and private basis; that this would be a step back from the fundamental principle that it is the duty of the state to educate its young children. Parenthetically, it may be said that the proposed measure met with defeat. When the opportunity came, "the lady" asked the mayor how many children were in the family, how many were incurable invalids, how many stupid, how many criminal, how many had in fact been obliged to sojourn in hospital, asylum or reformatory. The answer was, "None." Further inquiry proved that all these so-called "ruined" children were up with the average in intelligence, physical strength and social development. Unfortunately many such misleading statements regarding the kindergarden are allowed to pass unchallenged.

Reviewing the history of the elementary school during the past decade, an unbiased mind cannot fail to recognize that the kindergarten has proved the leaven which has not only brought new life and vitality to the primary school, but has stimulated interest in playgrounds, school gardens, story afternoons in public libraries, excursions to woods and parks, and other telling influences in child life. Its basic principles, too, have withstood the searching tests of modern psychology, biology and sociology in a manner which proves their soundness.   On this point, Doctor Irving King of the University of Iowa said at the International Kindergarten Union:

"It is always interesting for the advocates of any doctrine to see themselves in relation to the great world of thought that lies outside their particular sphere of action.   This is especially true if the broader view reveals this doctrine as vital and fundamental in its more remote as well as in its more immediate relations.

"All of the educational philosophies of the first half of the 19th century have had to be radically reconstructed in the light of the growing knowledge of the last twenty-five years.   It should be a satisfaction to the Kindergarten to know that Froebel's philosophy has suffered less in this direction than have any of the others   In many respects it seems that Froebel's educational conceptions have themselves been the dominant reconstructing factors, the centers about which the new educational philosophy has been and is being worked out.   They seem, in a word, to have furnished in many cases the clew to some of the most important of the recent developments in educational doctrine.   I am not prepared, however, to say just how far recent changes in point of view are to be traced directly to the influence of Froebel.   I do know that some of the most virile thinkers of the present day owe much directly, both in the way of point of view and of stimulus, to Froebel." [1]

[1] The Kindergarten Magazine, May, 1912, p. 240.

STORY TELLING TIME IN THE KINDERGARTEN.

While most American educators would agree to this psychologist's estimate of underlying principles, the practice of the kindergarten is subjected to sharp criticism, not only among patrons, but among superintendents and grade teachers as well. It is difficult to bear with these when they happen to be based upon ignorance or prejudice, or upon the unskilled and sentimental activities of the *lower one-sixth* group in connection with old and discarded occupation materials, long drawn out gift dictations, discussions of the Mother Play and other phases of kindergarten theory in technical terms, and quotation of mysterious passages from Froebel.

There is another type of criticism still more disturbing, which comes from both educators and patrons who are real friends of the movement. They recognize cause for anxiety in the kindergarten field among workers who possibly compose the *average* or *two-thirds* group. This is found in the sanguine attitude, the lack of acquaintance with the problems of the primary grades, the limited knowledge of advance movements in matters that affect children, the effort to bring children up to adult standards by the use of subject matter which is beyond them, and the reluctance to give up traditional methods of procedure in kindergarten work even though these are not in line with the best of modern insight. Every kindergartner should read the address on "Some Hopes and Fears for the Kindergarten," given recently by Professor Patty Smith Hill at the convention of the International Kindergarten Union in Washington. This far-seeing leader, after stating her reasons for profound faith in the kindergarten, offered splendid counsel regard-

o

ing "ways and means for building a more hopeful future."
She said in part:

"There are few changes in the nature and development of the
child as he passes from the kindergarten into the primary to justify

KINDERGARTEN CHILDREN WATCHING THE GOLDFISH.
(Iowa State Teachers College.)

the present separation and sharp distinctions between the two.
The period from four to eight is practically one, and our school
systems should unite the corresponding grades by training teachers

for kindergarten and primary together, so that a teacher may be prepared to teach the child anywhere from his fourth to his seventh or eighth year. The results of such a unification would be equally beneficial. The primary training would sift out of the kindergarten many activities which have crept into its procedure — activities which have little or no educational value and persist from tradition. While making the child temporarily happy, they lead nowhere, and the child would be equally happy and much better employed in other directions. On the other hand, the spirit of the kindergarten which has brought a life-giving element into education would pervade the grades to a far greater extent, bringing happiness to both teachers and children, and a freedom from an overloaded curriculum which makes children look back upon the kindergarten as the happiest period in their education.

"Is the reputation we have as a body of teachers separate and apart from education altogether unjust? Whether true or not, we have impressed people as blind followers of the past, as fetish worshipers, loyally clinging to one leader as the sole authority for all truth. It is largely due to our endless quotation of Froebel, on any and every problem of education and life, that Froebel, worthy of the deepest respect, is coming to be smiled upon as the educational idol of a deluded following of women; that the kindergarten is coming to be looked upon as 'the home of lost causes,' and 'impossible loyalties.' Our lack of perspective in defending those aspects of Froebel's work which science and common sense have disproved are sufficient reasons for Matthew Arnold's criticism of Oxford being applied to the kindergarten as 'a sanctuary in which exploded systems and obsolete prejudices find shelter and protection after they have been hunted out of every corner of the world.' Froebel does not merit such treatment, but we should not blame others for this. On the contrary, we should put ourselves to the test. Are we broad in our educational interests; are we willing to merge ourselves into the larger whole of education, even at the cost of yielding many of our traditions, our philosophical lingo, our technical terms which separate us from other teachers? Would we be willing to yield such purely 'kindergartenish' terms as 'gifts,' 'occupations,' 'life,' 'beauty,' and 'knowledge forms,' the kindergarten 'program,' and many other of like nature, if in so doing we unified our work with those in the elementary school along the same line?   Could we forego our own individual name, if by so doing we could eliminate the distance which now exists between the kindergarten and the school?   Why should we have to say 'the kindergarten and the school' any more than the primary and the school?   Education has developed from above downward, and primary education is a matter of recent universality — yet it has become so organic a part of the school that no one thinks of saying the primary and the school.   One includes primary as an integral part of the school.   Is this equally true of kindergarten, and are we willing to make any righteous sacrifice to bring this to pass?

"When we are willing to lay aside every dead weight of tradition, and the educational sins which so easily beset us, then the limitations of the kindergarten will be acknowledged and outgrown, and the best in Froebel will be so deeply rooted in both the kindergarten and the school, that the eternal verities for which it stands will live as a vital force in all education even if every kindergarten, so-called, existing as an institution separate and apart from education as a whole, should fade from memory." [1]

If the broad-minded attitude expressed by Miss Hill becomes prevalent among kindergarten workers, the sacrifice she mentions will not be called for.

In the recent New York City school inquiry, Professor Frank M. McMurry of Columbia University was the one appointed to make an investigation regarding the quality of teaching, the course of study and the supervision of the elementary schools.   This report, resulting from facts taken at first hand, is just published.   It is based upon standards in connection with four factors:

[1] Kindergarten Review, September, 1913, pp. 15–21.

1st.   Motive on the part of the pupils.

2d.   Weighing of values on the part of the pupils.

3d.   Organization of ideas by pupils.

4th.   Initiative by pupils.

The method of judging took into account the following:

"The original ability of the teacher is only one of the things that determine the quality of classroom instruction. The abilities of her superior officers are, likewise, important factors. The curriculum is a great aid or an obstacle to good results, according to the insight shown in selecting its subject matter; the syllabi, which interpret this curriculum and offer suggestions on method, are a guide and a source of inspiration or depression to teachers according to the definiteness of statement and the breadth of view that they evince; and, finally, the supervision by principals and superintendents tends to produce an enthusiasm that will manifest itself outside of school in extra preparation, and in the class by alertness to each pupil's condition; or it tends in the opposite direction. These other influences, taken together, must very greatly affect the atmosphere that surrounds the teacher. Without their positive support instruction can hardly be good; and, if they are doing their work fairly well, instruction is not likely to be poor." [1]

The results secured by the application of these standards, and the consideration of these conditions in New York kindergartens, are probably a fair estimate of the kindergarten situation in most of the large cities in America, where, close to the great universities and training school centers, the best prepared teachers are found. These would probably fall within the *excellent one-sixth* group of our normal curve. The far-reaching signifi-

[1] Elementary School Standards, Frank M. McMurry, pp. 55-56. School Efficiency Series, edited by Paul H. Hanus, published by World Book Co., Yonkers-on-Hudson, New York.

cance of this estimate is that it comes from a leader in the educational world who views the kindergarten with a better perspective than would be credited to one within the ranks. Here follows a portion of the report.

INSTRUCTION IN THE KINDERGARTEN

INCULCATION OF PURPOSES IN CHILDREN

Specific and childlike aims tending to call out a high degree of effort are very prominent in the kindergartens. A certain form is folded to serve as the mount for mother's valentine, to be presented at the valentine party of the Mothers' Meeting; a bag is folded and sewed, to be used in the postman's game; . . .

These detailed purposes play directly into the broader aims that are plainly in evidence in the kindergarten. Such are: a love of stories, of plants and animals, of games, of objects of beauty, and of constructive work — a love that finds expression in little deeds such as those named, and that leads to more far-reaching hopes and plans.

ATTENTION TO ORGANIZATION

Most kindergartners endeavor to organize the more or less random and instinctive activities of even their youngest children. At the kindergarten age the organization of ideas takes place largely through the organization of activity, the ordered act being considered the very best evidence of ordered thought. A representative play is worked out bit by bit, until a reasonably finished whole results; . . . all such efforts call for organization in the same sense as does the high school student's essay. The children are less conscious of the process, but they profit by it just as truly. One seldom visits a kindergarten without observing that the kindergartner herself is carrying the idea of organization constantly in mind, and without observing also that the children are doing the same thing, to some extent, in their attention to sequence, to the interrelation of facts, and to grouping.

Indeed, one of the most serious faults of the kindergarten is found in its over-devotion to sequence, particularly to the logical sequence of the adult, which is probably even more a source of torment to some children in the kindergarten than to any in the elementary school. . . .

But while there are such excesses here and there, we are convinced that on the whole an emphasis is placed upon organization of ideas in the kindergarten that is generally in accord with the worth placed upon it in life outside.

ATTENTION TO RELATIVE VALUES — IMAGINATION AND REASONING

The kindergarten makes noticeable provision for relative values. Emotional response, appreciation, preservation of an inquiring attitude of mind, socialized behavior, seem to be regarded in the regular instruction as of at least equal importance with knowledge. The general viewpoint of the kindergartner is that whatever is done in the kindergarten is of value to the extent that it counts, or functions, in life. Hence the tendency to weigh worth is common here, with both teachers and children.

Again, however, a defect is to be noted; namely, an extreme devotion on the teacher's part to technique, to precision, and to exact imitation now and then, which tends to influence the children to forget all about the real worth of things. This is true particularly in the use of materials, and is not representative of the work as a whole.

PROVISION FOR INITIATIVE AND INDEPENDENCE

Kindergarten teachers have an enviable opportunity for encouraging the exercise of initiative and individuality of children, because uniformity is not demanded. Without a fixed program and without rigid requirements of accomplishment, there is every incentive for teachers to allow pupils to do original and creative work; and this opportunity is not lost. It is common for children to set up aims, to organize their activities, to suggest subject matter or experience that forms the basis for their play and work, to choose songs, stories, games, and materials, and to lead in many of the undertakings.

While this seems to be the dominant tendency, it is also evident that in quite a number of the kindergartens dictation exercises and ready-made play that require complete submission of the part of the pupil, are so prominent that they directly oppose self-expression and self-reliance.

On the whole, there are two very distinct currents observable in the kindergartens. The one represents a slavish devotion to the adult point of view in the selection of subject matter and to adult logic in its presentation, resulting in rigid organization, ignoring of relative values, and neglect of the child himself. The other shows the opposite tendencies. Which of these two shall finally prevail is a matter of grave concern, requiring the constant watchfulness of all who are especially interested in this field.

But at present we feel little hesitation in saying that the kindergarten, as a whole, meets the test of the four standards set up in a satisfactory manner; and that therefore the instruction there rests on the higher plane, *i.e.* it is good at present and promising for the future.[1]

Judging the kindergarten and primary school of to-day by their *best* standards, how do they resemble, how do they differ from, how shall they be improved by, the Montessori school?

First. There is resemblance in the underlying ideas in regard to the child's, the teacher's, and the curriculum's contribution to the process of education. The child is a center of outgoing energy which makes him more than a passive recipient of impressions from his environment; he is an active acquirer of it. His equipment of tendencies to physical movements of all sorts and the accompanying activity of the sense organs have already been

[1] Elementary School Standards, Frank M. McMurry, pp. 56–59.

elaborated in previous talks. This results in the acquisition of coördinations that constitute the elemental control of his own body and of his environment, both human and natural. These prerequisites are gradually organized on higher levels as they function with tendencies that later take turns in becoming decidedly prominent. Among these are the impulse to collect and arrange things; to be curious about the what, how and why of objects and processes; to put into objective form through gesture, speech, drawing, making models and dramatic play, what has been gained through the earlier manipulation and imitation; to seek others of similar ages for companionship which eventually arrives at coöperative effort.

Second. They stand upon common ground when they insist that the child's constant contribution of impulsive instinctive activity must be utilized in the educative method. They differ, however, in their emphasis upon the impulses enumerated; for example, where the American primary school and kindergarten considers dramatic representation in connection with reading, literature and games very vital, it is given less attention in the Children's House.

Third. They agree when they maintain that the teacher's responsibility is twofold: (a) To be aware through observation of the child as an individual. The child will be manifesting these impulses somewhat in the form, time and order that all normal children of his class and age indicate them, and because of the similar heritage of "humanness"; somewhat, too, out of that form, time and order because of his peculiar white or yellow,

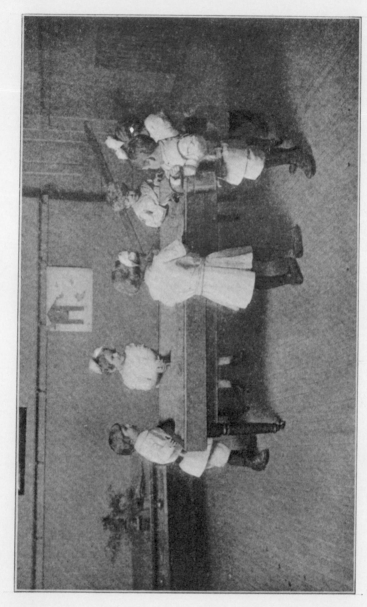

THE SAND TABLE — A NEVER-FAILING SOURCE OF DELIGHT.
(Iowa State Teachers College.)

English or Chinese, Brown and Jones, or San Foy and Sing Ling inheritance and environment. (*b*) To place within the child's environment those materials which will not only satisfy the manifested impulse through encouraging its function, but will do it with material that is desirable because it is not antagonistic to the trend of accepted social values.   These two considerations in relation to the selection of subject matter were recently stated thus :

1. "The curriculum of the school shall represent the needs and interests of present day life in our own immediate environment and the world at large — the social factor.

2. " The work at any given stage of a child's development shall be that which is adapted to the immediate enrichment of his life as measured by his individual needs and capacities — the psychological factor." [1]

Having in mind these two balancing factors, the psychological and social, we find that the schools vary in their selection of subject matter for children between the ages of three and six somewhat according to the following outline which is not offered as a complete grouping of subject matter but rather as a suggestive basis of comparison which may stimulate study and criticism. In such a comparative study the recent report of the Committee of Nineteen on " The Theory and Practice of the Kindergarten " will be found valuable in conjunction with Doctor Montessori's text — The Montessori Method.[2]

[1] The Speyer School Curriculum.   Teachers College, Columbia University, 1913.

[2] The Kindergarten, by Susan Blow, Patty Hill, Elizabeth Harrison. Houghton, Mifflin Company.

THE CHILDREN'S HOUSE	THE KINDERGARTEN AND PRIMARY SCHOOL
1. Practical Life.	
a. Care of the body, partial dressing.	*a, b, c*. Exceptional rather than common.
b. Actual care of rooms.	
c. Actual serving and clearing away of luncheon.	
2. Physical Education.	
a. Apparatus work for bodily poise, and for strengthening the larger muscles of legs, arms and trunk.	*a*. Rather unusual except for playground apparatus.
b. Exercises in standing, walking, sitting.	*b*. Incidental to other activities.
c. Organized games and free play.	*c*. Much the same with greater emphases upon dramatic and representative games.
3. Sense-training.	
a. Exercises with didactic materials.	*a*. Minimum amount.
b. Incidental exercises in general environment.	*b*. Scarcely any outside of situations directed toward other ends.
4. The Language Arts.	
a. The Three R's dealt with early.	*a*. All postponed to first grade. Tendency to postpone arithmetic to second or third grade.
b. Training in clear enunciation, good voice, correct speech.	
c. Some literature in form of stories.	*b, c, d*. Much the same with decided emphasis upon story telling.
d. Conversation.	

5. The   Constructive   and
Graphic Arts.
Modeling,   drawing,
water   colors   and
some construction.

All carry over with emphasis upon building and additions in the way of paper cutting, cardboard and wood construction.

6. Music.
Singing, rhythm. Training in voice quality and in appreciation through listening to choice music.

Similar.

7. Ethics.
   a. Direct conversations on behavior.

   a. Unusual.

   b. Indirect lessons in reverence, nurture and service through daily experience, *i.e.*
   Morning devotions
   Care of younger children
   Care of room
   Care of pets
   Gardening

   b, c. All carry over. (Usual.)

   c. Reverence and love for the beautiful and good stimulated by simple and childlike experiences with fundamental things in nature, art, scientific processes and social institutions.

It would be seen from these parallel columns that the points of greatest variance are those under "4," and it will at once occur to the student of the history of elementary work in this country that these features constituted at one time a large part of the material offered to the child before the age of seven. He will recognize, too, that when the kindergarten held forth the ideal of a curriculum enriched by hand work, games, physical exercise, gardening and stories, the primary

LITTLE BUILDERS IN THE KINDERGARTEN.
(Iowa State Teachers College.)

school was slow to respond, partly because of the nature of the educational conception of elementary school teachers, principals, superintendents, school boards, parents and other tax payers. This condition of affairs gave the kindergarten its first setback in practice, for it had to be cramped to meet and adjust itself to existing ideals and practices.   For recovery from this, it has had to wait, and is waiting, upon changes in the elementary school which are being brought about as the sociologist and psychologist throw new light upon children's capacities and needs.

When it comes to the comparison of the content of some of the subjects found in both curricula, one finds a similar correspondence between what once was and now is in kindergarten, primary school and Children's House, respectively. Holding the idea that one must proceed from the simple to the complex, Froebel, for instance, planned that drawing should develop from lines varying in length and direction, to their combination into angles, and angles into plane figures called forms of knowledge. The groups of lines, the angles and plane figures, were also arranged into designs or patterns called beauty forms.

The primary school at this same period was teaching reading by beginning with letters as the simplest (because smallest) element and proceeding to words, sentences, etc., as progressively more complex. It taught writing by finding still simpler elements in the parts of the letters. Practice upon them was followed by whole letters, words, etc. It is commonly acknowledged that this mode of procedure proved extremely laborious for children.

At the first glance, it would seem as though Doctor Montessori had followed the same principle and repeated these earlier efforts, for she does begin with the elements analyzed out of wholes; these are mastered in turn and then built up into the wholes. *But it must be borne in mind that she makes use of a vital source of information, the tactile-muscular sensory activity, concerning which the teachers of long ago were uninformed;* that she has writing precede reading; that both are acquired early and with an ease and speed that eliminate all drudgery, *and in an atmosphere so splendidly free from the strain of the military order of the oldtime primary school that the child's body, mind and spirit are pliable and responsive.*

CHAPTER X

OTHER AGENCIES OF EARLY EDUCATION — CONTINUED

THE comparison of the Children's House and the American kindergarten and primary school made thus far, grow out of the statement that the child, the teacher and the curriculum each have their peculiar contributions to make to the educative process. But these three factors have been considered apart from the feature of *method* — the manner in which the child and curriculum are brought together by the teacher. It is now almost a truism in educational discussions to say that the teacher's method of teaching is just the other aspect of the child's method of learning. But the child's methods, like those of the adult and of the race, are several.[1] Contact, manipulation, experimentation without aid and with aid and purpose, unconscious imitation of copy — these are all necessary and legitimate ways of coming to know objects, people and processes. With these as basic apperceptive materials, the child can also learn through looking at pictures and listening to and reading the words of others. In fact, were his acquisition limited by what he could experience directly, he would know but little beyond the span of his own generation and locality.

Now the teacher's method must therefore be one of

---

[1] Kindergarten Problems, MacVannels.

"methods." She must know the appropriate time, place and number of educative situations in which direct and indirect experiences shall predominate or fuse and in which she must be relatively passive and active. No one will deny that the older primary school was a place in which indirect experiencing and activity of the teacher were overwhelmingly in evidence. The balance to-day is undoubtedly, so far as the elementary school is concerned, somewhat in favor of things and processes and of the child's activity. This is a combination for which the kindergarten has stood from the beginning; this is embodied also in the Children's House.

It is probable that no passages in the "Education of Man" have been more misunderstood and ridiculed than the following:

"Therefore, education . . . should necessarily be passive, following (only guarding and protecting), not prescriptive, categorical, interfering."

"This necessity implies that the young human being — as it were, still in the process of creation — would seek, although still unconsciously, as a product of nature, yet decidedly and surely, that which is in itself best; and, moreover, in a form wholly adapted to his condition, as well as to his disposition, his powers, and means."

"We grant space and time to young plants and animals because we know that, in accordance with the laws that live in them, they will develop properly and grow well; young animals and plants are given rest, and arbitrary interference with their growth is avoided, because it is known that the opposite practice would disturb their pure unfolding and sound development; but the young human being is looked upon as a piece of wax, a lump of clay, which man can mold into what he pleases." [1]

[1] The Education of Man, Froebel, pp. 7–8. D. Appleton & Co.

There has probably been no aspect of work like that
embodying the ideas of Dr. John Dewey at the Elementary School of the University of Chicago which has

A SINGING GROUP IN THE KINDERGARTEN.
(Iowa State Teachers College.)

received as caustic criticism as has the idea of giving
the child the privilege of being the active agent in his
own education. Doctor Montessori exhorts teachers

to a policy of self-effacement that has much in common with the views presented by such experimental schools. Whether her practice would go beyond what was in the minds of these reformers and probably approximated by some of their associates, it would be impossible to say. Her directresses are to intervene only when the children's acts are antisocial, ill-bred, or harmful, when they (so far as didactic materials are concerned) are not in accordance with the most direct route to the accomplishment of their specific purposes. She would not permit a child to mar furniture, or to snatch an object from another, since the materials were intended for other purposes, to walk down the stairs made by him out of the broad blocks, or to use the long stair rods to construct railroad tracks. With all but the last two of these the kindergarten and primary school would agree. But with these, the variance would be that uses which enrich the child's experience with what he has made, or that add to his discovery of the possibilities of the material composing it, are encouraged. There is never just one, or a very limited number of things that can be done with the handwork materials used in kindergarten and primary school. Since Doctor Montessori, however, provides some material to supplement the didactic set, one can imagine that the equipment, when not limited by funds, will resemble somewhat the equipment of the kindergarten which has acquired the didactic apparatus. At least some of the Froebelian materials objected to by Doctor Montessori are those now obsolete in the best American kindergarten practice.

Through the self-effacement of the teacher and the

provision for movable furniture, the child is to grow in self-help and independence as he has not grown before. This doctrine, too, is held by the kindergarten, but the exigencies of being obliged to dismiss some thirty children and to come back from luncheon in an hour or so to play and work with another thirty children necessitates some helping with wraps that is not in accord with the theory of the one who does the helping. The conception that the time schedule of a very short session (instead of an all day one) must guide the changes of work for the group, may also be productive in practice of more assistance than the kindergarten teacher approves of.   The time schedule exists in the Children's House, but it does not force itself upon the attention of the visitor so decidedly for two reasons: first, because of the longer day; and second, because for certain periods (sense-exercises, hand work, gardening) the children are not in groups arranged by the teacher on the basis of the children's apparently similar capacities.

The plan of individual work is one of the most valuable features of the Montessori school.   It must be borne in mind, however, that the group activities of the really good American kindergarten and primary school bring valuable experiences to children.   For example, having given material to a group, the teacher looks for variations in the reactions upon the same.   If colored crayons and paper are given for the first time, the teacher will see some helter-skelter scribbling, some smooth rubbing, some orderly arrangement of lines or dots, some representations of objects.   When the appropriate moment arrives, she encourages a sharing of the

EXPLORATION AND DISCOVERY — THE GREENHOUSE.

(Iowa State Teachers College.)

results.   She or the children or both show papers to the class, telling what has happened. She comments, possibly, upon the one which has upon it the effort for which she wishes the class to strive, basing her wish upon her knowledge of the subject matter of drawing (both representative and decorative) and her knowledge of the children's ability.

With papers passed, the class sets to work again.

This time those who were ready for the next step will show the influence of the moment or two that was given to looking and listening. Suppose that smooth colorings of the surface had been chosen for emphasis by the teacher ; the second crop of papers would show a greater number with efforts at smooth surface covering. Sometimes the result will suggest to the child its resemblance to something well known to him. Immediately his effort becomes that thing, and he then wishes paper to attempt more of the same. The round and round red spots of good size may have suggested apples ; the horizontal green or brown spots, the grass or ground ; the blue, the sky or water. But ere long by accident or by idea he places more in his pictures ; the apple must be on a tree, the tree must have ground under it and sky above it.   As level after level is reached, he and his group are made conscious of each other's efforts and results. This pooling is never for the attainment of absolute uniformity of ideas, of composition and of technique. It is for the enrichment and defining of experience.

Some of these results are placed on the bulletin board for a brief time where all may see them ; some are selected for the books which the children will eventually take home — not only to show to parents but to remind themselves of their growth in skill; some will be used to decorate the blotter, the calendar, the booklet, or card with which the children plan to mark the festivals of Christmas, Valentine and Easter. These with the furnishing of play houses, the making of simpler toys or utensils, lift the child's activity to the level of the purposive; a level on which he conceives a desired end, selects materials and determines the process necessary to its realization. This, the nature of work at its best, is also the nature of play. The two activities are not antagonistic, as some would suppose. Both satisfy fundamental human needs; both can embody the same mental attitude. If each is worth its name, they are entered into with equal zest, curiosity and ambition for skillful performance.

In the sweep of the movement from first scribbling to an art production of gift book, or toy house furnishing, what the children have accomplished will be supplemented by looking at or hearing about what the teacher or a greater artist than she has accomplished. The teacher has been guided by the principle that "as a usual thing, no activity should begin with the imitation of an adult model." This principle holds true in the use of various materials for hand work, games, and stories. At luncheon, the children do the best they can in passing the paper napkins, the glass of water and the graham wafers; they eat and drink as daintily as they have been trained to do in the home. Of course, they watch each other and the teacher. They absorb much copy, and sometimes consciously, often unconsciously, they modify their own actions. The teacher's, "I am glad Helen broke her bread before taking any of it," defines a particularly good effort on a child's part; the other children's attention is centered upon it for a moment, it becomes a standard toward which those who are ready will aspire at their next opportunity.

This profiting by each other's experience through the organized group work, and this greater use of the better things that children of varying ages, abilities and home training will contribute are marked features of our best kindergarten and primary schools. It is sometimes a shorter cut than that involved in purely individual instruction, as it keeps the standard (or model) close to the child's ability; there is also opportunity for individual work in the good kindergarten and primary school. The writer observed some group work in the Children's Houses delightfully carried out, but the didactic materials as far as noticed were not used until they had been presented to individual children, through individual lessons. The presentation consisted in doing (and saying) just the one or few things for which the material was designed. The cylindrical insets were not to be rolled as barrels or built up into a tower or to march as soldiers, but were to be taken out and put back into the frame. The elimination of error, the decrease of time, the association of thick, thicker; thin, thinner, with the perception of variation in dimension, and the deft handling as the cylinders were replaced into the frame, were goals sought. The experimentation to find new possibilities of material, the play of the imagina-

KINDERGARTEN CHILDREN USING MONTESSORI MATERIALS.

(Iowa State Teachers College.)

tion, clothing the objects with other attributes, were evidences that the child was not ready for, or had mastered, what the apparatus involved. In either case, he and it were separated.

The free-hand drawing (without use of metal insets), some of the clay work, and blocks of various kinds, afford the child opportunities for effort without the copy being shown or dictated. There might be danger here, if one were not skilled in keeping the proper balance, of swinging from extreme prescription of copy by an adult on the one hand to absence of guidance on the other. Since invention and imitation are the two legs upon which the race has walked in reaching its present level of æsthetic, industrial and institutional life, and since every normal human being is constantly exhibiting in his own early life (and later, if he hasn't allowed himself to fall into a rut) the tendency to walk similarly, good method in kindergarten, primary school and Children's House must seek to embrace in the most helpful proportion for the individual and the group the elements of discovering and of copying.

To elaborate all the points of similarity and difference between the agencies under discussion is not the purpose of this book. Its aim is rather to provoke investigation and the testing out and measuring of our own and other's methods by the best standards that can be set up.

Doctor Montessori has satirized the Italian kindergarten, with its small unventilated rooms, its large numbers (50 or more in the care of one teacher), its long, slanting desks and benches, its tiresome dictated occupations and directed games ; and her statements have been seized upon and made capital of by those who are opposed to the kindergarten. If she has for her background and the basis of her judgments the sort of municipal kindergartens which the writer saw in Rome, her criticisms are well taken. It is likely that Doctor Montessori has little conception of kindergarten procedure as carried on in a *good* American school. A careful study of her book and observations of her methods as applied with children in Rome, would prompt one to believe that she would find much to delight her in our American child garden, with its elusive, changeable materials, its childlike dramatic play, its rich social experiences, its space, sunshine and hygienic care, its artistic, simple surroundings.

No one who reads her book and is stirred by the wise judgment and deep spiritual insight there conveyed, can accuse Doctor Montessori of ignoring the creative and imaginative sides of a child's nature, although these are not emphasized in her system. She is preëminently a scientist, and as one might expect, the trend of her plans is toward the practical, the clear-cut, the fact side as a foundation. In her dealings with children, however, the tender, nurturing, human spirit is most evident. She has come into sudden and unsought prominence in the educational world and has been forced to display a system not yet perfectly completed or rounded out.

Elizabeth Harrison tells us that it is a mark of culture to refuse to pass judgment upon a thing not fully understood. We should be open-minded in our attitude toward the Casa dei Bambini, and feel a keen sense of fellowship with this woman across the water who has, with intellectual grasp and common sense, made a demonstration of some fundamental ideas among children of varying types and conditions. It is not necessary to agree with all these ideas in order to catch the inspiration and profit by the insight of Doctor Montessori. She stirs us to a firmer belief in the faith that is in us along such lines as (1) freedom for the child, (2) individual instruction, (3) auto-education, (4) suitable stimuli for sensory activity, (5) a simplified schedule, (6) care of the child's body, (7) patience, poise and lack of haste, (8) plenty of outdoor life.

If we gain a full conception of the significance of such school health ideals as Doctor Montessori has reannounced, many transformations will occur in school environment. Teachers will become more intelligent, more sensitive, more active; supervising officers will keep abreast with their teachers in all matters, so that they may not only be sanely sympathetic with requests made but may become aggressive through carefully compiled and publicly distributed information concerning existing conditions; school boards will be composed of men and women whose intelligence is equal to selecting, understanding and trusting for supervisory and teaching forces such persons as can give evidence of knowledge of and interest in the health aspect of school life; parents will come to a realization that their obligations entail a first-hand knowledge of the school to which they intrust their children, and will thus become willing to make greater sacrifices, if necessary, for the support of health-promoting schools.

Since the development of strong, vigorous children means more to America's future than the development of the choicest Burbank varieties of fruits, or the promotion of the greatest pecuniary enterprise, it is well for us to consider these matters.[1]

Doctor Montessori recommends, first, a wholesome school environment in which are provided suitable chairs instead of spine-curving seats, fresh air and sunshine, nourishing food and comfortable clothing; broad, open spaces and earth to dig in; plants to water and pets to feed, and, since physical strength like moral fiber comes only through actual struggle, gymnastic apparatus upon which growing bodies may stretch and balance. (This includes a suspended rubber ball to push for arm development, a fence for climbing, a spiral staircase, rope ladders and swings.[2])   Second, careful and frequent biological tests and measurements, made for the purpose of detecting and endeavoring to overcome every physical defect, thus freeing the child from handicap and protecting society against the possibility of weakness perpetuating itself through heredity.   Third, the child is taught scientific truth regarding his body and given definite instruction as to its care, which develops a reverence for it and tends toward personal purity and health. Fourth, through definite training in motor control and muscular coördination, tension is removed, and poise and serenity result.

Our American children, with their buoyancy of spirit and their fund of nervous energy, need careful attention along these lines.   The child's health rights should

[1] Manual of Mental and Physical Tests, Whipple.
[2] The Montessori Method, Chapter IX.

be placed in the foreground, and child hygiene, medical inspection and desirable school equipment and sanitation urged by teachers who must first become more intelligent themselves as to the close relationship between physical health and mental and moral vigor. Weekly conferences between parents and teachers will aid in this safeguarding.[1]

The coöperation of the church, the women's club, the Parent-teacher Association, and other organizations may reasonably be expected in the campaign for the stimulation of public sentiment along these lines.

Health assured, the child's next right is the opportunity to grow into an independent human being through the exercise of his own capacities on tasks that seem of great moment to him and at a rate of speed commensurate with his particular condition. There is the classic story of the American superintendent who proudly proclaimed that his school system was so perfected that he could tell at any moment just what every class of every grade was doing. Superintendents generally would not acknowledge such an ideal, but the goal suggested by the Children's Houses (that the time schedule and the choice of material are of secondary importance to the child's power and rate of growth, and interest in a given task) has seldom been striven for.

Some rural school teachers are now running on prescribed schedules of thirty recitations a day. To get them all in means keeping account of time and stopping whether children have arrived anywhere or not.[2]   Except

---

[1] Medical Inspection of Schools, Gulich and Ayers.
[2] The Country School, Seerley, p. 52.

for fewer recitations per day, the same statement is true of city school systems. Getting through according to the clock instead of the children seems the principle most in practice. The same is true when one thinks of that other time indicator — the calendar. The slow must be hurried on to reach the minimum for passing, the bright must be restrained from exceeding the maximum for promotion into the next grade; the pernicious, lock-step idea of the businesslike superintendent controlling not only the children's growth, but the teacher's ideals as well.[1]

Ayres throws much light upon this problem in his discussion of remedial measures.[2] He gives the report of one city school, where the schedule is so flexible that children move along from class to class in subject after subject as they individually can. Regularity of attendance, good health, faithful application to work, and natural endowment are each potent factors in determining how many years shall be spent in securing an education.

According to this report of those who enter the high school from the grammar school, 49 per cent have done the work in six years, 29 per cent have done the same in five years, 7 per cent in four years, and 15 per cent had to take the longer time of seven or more years. In this system, the bugaboo of administration of adjusting one school to another has not been allowed to overshadow their real purpose — the development and education of human beings. Just why such systems

[1] All the Children of All the People, Smith, Chapter XV.
[2] Laggards in Our Schools, Ayres, Russell Sage Foundation.

have not exerted more influence in this country it is difficult to explain. In such a system, the relation of teacher to pupil would necessarily be somewhat like that in the Children's House. It would be her business to observe individuals carefully, to keep a record of their progress, to pass the same along to the next teacher. It would be her business to provide a stimulating environment, to leave the child free in his reactions upon the same and to help him when he has reached his own limit or to prepare him for a conquest which would be time wasting if left to the individual. She would undoubtedly become *outwardly* much more passive, and *inwardly* much more active. She would do much less talking, and more thinking. She would be more direct, simple and concise when the moment for instruction arrived.

Coupled with the development of independence must be the training for service. In the Children's House, the medium for this is the activities usually carried on in the home, performed by paid caretakers in the school or acquired in the domestic economy element that is beginning to permeate American courses of study.

It is likely that nearly every phase of washing, dressing, serving luncheon, and caring for rooms is present in many schools in this country where these activities are needed as much as they were in the original Children's Houses. In some schools, especially of a philanthropic or private nature, such service to self and in turn to others is theoretically based on the idea of training for social service when it is, in reality, a necessary financial economy. The point at which such routine tasks lose

Q

their educative value must not be ignored. Other and newer thought-stimulating problems do present themselves to children and teachers, and time must be allowed for these. Education means doing new things, meeting unexpected emergencies and not continuously going over the same ground. If one would continue to grow, in later life, when one's occupation entails this repetition, there is especial need of fostering new interests.

Among the things bequeathed to every human being by the race, are, as well as the *content* of learning, the so-called *tools* of learning. The Children's House by changing the order of the two R's, and by using the tactile motor apparatus in acquiring writing before reading, eliminates drudging labor for the Italian child and puts in its place pleasant energy-saving activity.

The question as to when the child should learn to read and write is one upon which opinion varies. Most American authorities would have him wait until he has gained some acquaintance with his environment and had opportunity for self-expression through many natural childlike means, with the social motive in the foreground. Concerning this matter Elisabeth Ross Shaw recently said :

"In regard to the too early teaching of reading and writing, the unanimous testimony of biologists, neurologists and psychologists is, that certain fundamental parts of the brain develop first, and their accessory association areas mature later. Speech is fundamental, reading is accessory; drawing is fundamental, writing is accessory. Surely it is only common sense to exercise the earliest developed powers first, knowing that throughout organic evolution, from the lowest forms of life to its human apex, the higher functions are reached by development from the lower. To develop an accessory power prematurely is like pulling green fruit while leaving an abundant harvest of ripe fruit ungathered."[1]

To prove or disprove the value of the Montessori ideas and materials on such points involves some carefully conducted experiments. Up to now, there are no carefully measured results upon the education of children with varied materials and varying methods. The widespread interest in Doctor Montessori's work should lead to such experiments, well conducted. These would entail an outlay for equipment, for expert teachers and other workers far beyond that yet allowed for young children.

America's greatest need to-day is scientific insight on the part of those who have to do with the vital problem of race training. A proper biological, psychological and social background would bring wisdom and judgment to all matters of choice of method and material to be used in the educative process.

It is true that actual daily contact with children clears away many misconceptions, but scientific knowledge of the little body through which the soul is struggling for realization, and definite information as to the natural behavior of the potential mind and spirit gives to the parent or teacher a scientist's confidence and an artist's touch upon child life which results in bodily poise, intellectual mastery and social coöperation.

With this attitude, none would be blind followers of any system, method or device (be it that of Pestalozzi, Froebel or Montessori), but all would challenge each to measure up to standards set by the latest word from

[1] National Education Association Proceedings, 1913.

the science of child study. And regarding the theory and practice of any institution where little children are taught (home, kindergarten, primary school, or Casa dei Bambini) such questions as the following, and many others, would be asked:

1. Does it call for alert intelligence on the part of adults regarding the childish instincts, tendencies and needs which take turns in becoming prominent during these years? *i.e.* to investigate, to imitate, to construct, to nurture, to wonder, to control, etc.

2. Do the materials offered provide suitable nourishment for these hungering instincts while they at the same time exert an influence toward socialized conduct? *i.e.* Montessori didactic and gymnastic apparatus, kindergarten gifts and occupations, playground equipment, household activities, manual training, books, weights and measures, gardens, pets, stories, music, conversation, dramatization, games, drawing, writing, nature study, elementary science, social institutions, etc.

3. Are these stimuli placed within the child's reach by the adult in such a manner that he spontaneously responds to them and thus becomes an active agent in his own development? *i.e.*

a. Are the child's tastes, abilities and previous experiences so considered that the aims are childlike and natural?

b. Are the incipient powers of judgment and choice brought into exercise?

c. Is opportunity given for freedom (not caprice) which is balanced by responsibility, thus stimulating initiative, independence and self-control?

d. Is there a tendency toward clear thinking, and toward the organization of ideas and activities?

e. Do activities tend toward self-directed and creative effort, and is the child happy in his work because it seems to him worthy of his effort (not monotonous drudgery) and because he can recognize and correct his own mistakes when they are pointed out?

f. Does the day's program hold the child's health as a supreme consideration, viewing subject matter in its relation to mental and physical fatigue?

g. Is the spirit of curiosity and wonder in regard to things in nature turned to account as the beginning of reverence and faith?

It is to be hoped that Montessori ideals will find their place in American life in a natural and unforced way, that such workers as Miss George and others who have had the good fortune to study with Doctor Montessori will so adapt her methods as to make them valuable for our uses, and that all parents and teachers who attempt to apply the methods and materials in home and school will do so with that respect for the fundamental principles underlying them which will bring (1) reverence for personality and (2) recognition of the immeasurable educative possibilities of the young child.

The more flexible day and term, the greater emphasis upon individual progress, the more gradual group organization, the more self-effacing adult, the more intelligent provision for sensori-motor activity and other valuable features may be tried out within the usual limits set by average home and school requirements.

A careful consideration of the Montessori Method will

convince all those who seek to be fair and candid
that it contains principles of vital worth and that the
schools offer object lessons which we cannot afford to
ignore.   While there is not yet in sight any such thing

NIMBLE FINGERS LACING A MONTESSORI FRAME.
(Iowa State Teachers College.)

as finality in educational systems, and while we are not
looking for systems as such, let us hope that in the
changing and eddying currents of our study and experiment, we shall gradually receive and assimilate the
best in each new conquest of thought.   Here, in America, the very spirit of our democratic society has brought

to pass much of the freedom, the self-activity and the personal development which Doctor Montessori has embodied in a coherent system.   It is not likely that we shall see any clear line of cleavage between the old and the new, but we shall no doubt see in time the introduction of every demonstrated principle of The Montessori Method, which shall help children to escape unnecessary drudgery, and to find the acquisition of truth and power a process of delight.

BIBLIOGRAPHY

The Montessori Method, by Maria Montessori.
   Translated from the Italian by Anne E. George.
      Frederick A. Stokes Co., New York, Publishers, 1912, 377 pp.
      An illuminating treatise of theory and practice. A neces-
      sary text for the student of Dr. Montessori's system.
Pedagogical Anthropology, by Maria Montessori.
   Translated from the Italian by Frederick Taber Cooper.
      Frederick A. Stokes Co., New York, Publishers, 1913, 508 pp.
      This large volume, composed of lectures delivered at the
      University of Rome during a period of four years, is the
      result of deep scientific research and will prove an invaluable
      guide to those students wishing to gain a mastery of the
      basic principles underlying the Montessori Method.
The Montessori System, by Theodate L. Smith.
      Harper & Bros., New York, Publishers, 1912, 78 pp.
      A brief but clear explanation of the pedagogic methods of
      Dr. Maria Montessori from the standpoint of a psychologist
      and practical worker with children, including an account
      of some experiments made in an American school.
A Montessori Mother, by Dorothy Canfield Fisher.
      Henry Holt and Company, New York, Publishers, 1912,
         238 pp.
      Mrs. Fisher, disclaiming all attempt at technical discussion,
      psychological or pedagogical, brings to American mothers
      and teachers an inspirational message regarding the ideals
      and practices of Dr. Montessori.
         The charmed reader finds herself watching the activities
      of Montessori children and entering with joyous relish
      into every one of them, because of the graceful style, the

nurturing sympathy and wisdom, the subtle humor and the vivid illustrations of truth brought by this skillful writer.

A Guide to the Montessori Method, by Ellen Yale Stevens.

Frederick A. Stokes Co., New York, Publishers, 1913, 240 pp. A co prehensive study of the psychological basis of Dr. Montessori's method and a summary and interpretation of the principles underlying it. Also a study of "their concrete embodiment" in the didactic materials with suggestions for amplification and adaptation in the United States and a description of a successful summer experiment with a group of American children.

The Montessori System of Education, by Anna Tolman Smith.

U. S. Bureau of Education Bulletin, 1912, No. 17, 30 pp. An explanation of characteristic features set forth in the Montessori Method, with some comments from other authors and a discussion of the applicability of the Method in the United States.

The Normal Child and Primary Education, by Beatrice C. & Arnold Gesell.

Ginn & Co., Boston, Publishers, 1912. An appendix gives 18 pages to the discussion of the Montessori Method under the title, The Montessori Kindergarten.

National Educational Association Proceedings, 1912, pp. 609–621.

National Educational Association Proceedings, 1913, Kindergarten Department.

American Primary Teacher, Vol. 35, pp. 285–286, April 1912. Editorial, Dr. A. E. Winship. Gives in sententious style a fair, clear-cut statement of "What the Montessori system is," "What the Montessori system is not," "What the Montessori system does."

American Primary Teacher, Vol. 35, pp. 368–369, June 1912. Mary Jackson Kennedy. The author sees in the Montessori method "Strong forces to reform many evils of our present system and much to supplement kindergarten work." She is not, however, an "advocate of the method as an educational cure-all." Experiments made at Miss Wheeler's school, Providence, R.I., are briefly referred to.

Contemporary Review, Vol. 102, p. 328, September 1912.
Spontaneous Education. Herbert Burrows.
A thoughtful and appreciative article.

Current Literature, Vol. 52, pp. 311–313, March 1912.
A Movement to Revolutionize Education. Editorial.
A discussion of the American school problem. More democratic and libertarian education urged, and the ideals of Montessori and Ferrer held up as contributions to this end.

Delineator.
Vol. 83, No. 4, October 1913.
Began a series of articles by Carolyn Sherwin Bailey. Suggestions as to the application of the method in the home. Miss Bailey has studied the schools in Rome.

Dial, Vol. 52, pp. 392–394, May 16, 1912.
The Montessori Method of Teaching. M. V. O'Shea.
Contrasts Montessori and the American methods, and concludes with the statement, "The whole Montessori system is about where the American system was twenty-five years ago. It is a great improvement on general Italian practice in Rome, but it does not give the American teacher a new point of view which will be of service to him in solving his present problems."

Education, Vol. 33, pp. 1–10, September 1912.
The Montessori Methods. W. H. Holmes.
The writer claims that "Montessori with her communizing ideas, is sowing the seeds of a doctrine which leads away from the home." He refers to the Children's Houses where the motherly care of the children is communized, and says, "So far as I can see, the spiritual mother element is lacking to a large degree in the Montessori method."

Elementary School Teacher, Vol. 12, pp. 253–258. February 1912.
Montessori and Froebel — A Comparison. Ellen Yale Stevens.

From the standpoint of a Montessori advocate, Miss Stevens points out that "As Maria Montessori's preparation was so much broader than that of Froebel, as her genius — creative and intuitive like his — had a severer, more scientific training, so is the point of view of each essentially different." "While Froebel sees first the universe, then the child, Montessori's point of view is wholly that of the child." "Froebel's teachers are in front of their children" — leading, directing. "Montessori's are behind theirs, watching" — leaving initiative to the children.

Elementary School Teacher, Vol. 13, pp. 66–79, October 1912.

Montessori and Froebelian Methods and Materials. L. A. Palmer.

The author discusses from a kindergartner's standpoint the possible combinations of Montessori and Froebelian materials and methods as suggested by Professor Holmes in his introduction to "The Montessori Method."

"It would seem as though the Montessori and Froebelian materials were not equivalent, that they were intended to supplement each other. One lays emphasis on a single property of matter at a time, the other offers several for discrimination and consideration. One draws attention to the inert properties of matter which pertain to lower forms of nature, the other includes motion and possible position, the attributes of higher types of life. Montessori emphasizes the more primitive attitude of the child as a learner from material, Froebel suggests experimenting and learning from material but also using it to carry out human ideas."

"Mme. Montessori is restricted in materials and methods with materials, but she is free in actual practice because she feels so intensely the individual's right to follow his own life. Froebel's materials and possible methods are freer, but when he described his practice he became more circumscribed."

"Choice might be based upon the degree to which the materials carry out the characteristic aims of the two educators, the discovery and control of the properties of matter, and the interpretation through material. This is a question which admits of much debate."

Good Housekeeping Magazine, Vol. 55, pp. 24–29.

Dr. Maria Montessori — An Account of the Achievements and Personality of an Italian Woman whose Discovery is revolutionizing Educational Methods. Anne E. George.

Interesting because of Miss George's close acquaintance with Dr. Montessori and her work.

International Review of Missions, April 1913.

Montessori Method and Missionary Methods. Allen Roland.

Journal of Education has the following articles written by well-known American educators.

Vol. 76, p. 39, July 4, 1912.

A Caution on Montessori. Lightner Witmer.

Vol. 77, p. 63, January 16, 1913.

A Valuation of the Montessori Experiments. Walter M. Halsey.

Results of some definite experiments in the use of materials are here given, and the author states: "Dr. Montessori has given us valuable suggestions — yes, even a challenge, but not a model to take as a whole." "To know her one must understand her central organizing idea — it is freedom."

Vol. 77, p. 147, February 6, 1913.

The Conflicting Pedagogy of Madame Montessori. W. A. Baldwin.

Claims that the freedom promised is not provided because of the prescribed use of artificial didactic materials.

Vol. 77, p. 328, March 1913.

A Montessori Experiment in Maine.

Tells of the successful use of the didactic materials.

Vol. 77, p. 538, May 15, 1913.

Seguin's Principles of Education as Related to the Montessori Method. Katrina Myers.

A discussion of the theories and materials of Seguin set forth by a student of the abnormal child. The steps in the educative process as laid down by Seguin in his "Idiocy, Its Treatment by a Physiological Method," and carried out by him in actual practice, are explained, and points of similarity between these and the Montessori method are indicated.

Journal of Educational Psychology. 3 : 121–32. March 1912. Howard C. Warren. A praiseworthy review of the work done in the Montessori schools. From the standpoint of a psychologist.

Kindergarten Primary Magazine has the following series of excellent articles by Dr. Jennie B. Merrill.

Vol. 22, pp. 106–107, December 1909.

Vol. 22, pp. 142–144, January 1910.

Vol. 22, pp. 211–212, February 1910.

Vol. 22, pp. 297–298, March 1910.

Vol. 24, pp. 96–98, December 1911.

Valuable articles by Dr. W. N. Hailman are found in the same magazine.

Vol. 24, pp. 261–263, June 1912.

A Glimpse of the Montessori Method.

Vol. 25, pp. 6–7, September 1912.

The Montessori Method and the Kindergarten.

Kindergarten Review, Vol. 23, No. 8, April 1913.

Contains short, pertinent articles from three psychologists which discuss the relation of the Montessori Method to American school conditions.

Kindergarten Review, Vol. 23, pp. 553–561, May 1912.

Montessori and Froebel. Anna E. Logan.

Ladies' Home Journal, Vol. 29, p. 30, November 1913.

What Really is the Montessori Method?

Author says that kindergartens will have much to unlearn before undertaking the Montessori Method, because "they must avoid stimulating the child's imagination and let it wake of its own motion."

McClure's Magazine was the first periodical to present the Montessori Method to American readers and has contributed the following authentic articles, written by Dr. Montessori herself and by other women who have come into personal touch with her schools. *McClure's Magazine* has now a regularly established department — The Montessori Movement — conducted by Ellen Yale Stevens who, conversant with every phase of Montessori work both abroad and in America, is able to answer questions and give the latest word connected with the movement.

Vol. 37, pp. 3–19, May 1911.
An Educational Wonder Worker. Josephine Tozier.

Vol. 38, pp. 122–137, January 1912.
Montessori Schools in Rome. Josephine Tozier.

Vol. 38, pp. 289–302.
A Description of the Materials and Apparatus Used in Teaching by the Montessori Method. Josephine Tozier.

Vol. 39, pp. 95–102, May 1912.
Disciplining Children. Maria Montessori.
Doctor Montessori's own account of her manner of developing that kind of active discipline which leads to self-control.

Vol. 39, pp. 177–187, June 1912.
First Montessori School in America. Anne E. George.
Miss George was Mme. Montessori's first American pupil and the first teacher to apply the Montessori method in the United States. The successful experiment was made in Tarrytown, New York.

Vol. 40, pp. 77–82, November 1912.
Montessori Method and the American Kindergarten. Ellen Yale Stevens.
Discusses the relative merits of the two systems. Declares that Montessori has gone deeper than Froebel.

Vol. 41, No. 1, May 1913.
Rhythm Work in the Children's House at Washington. Anne E. George.

New York Teachers Monographs, Vol. 14, pp. 25–32, June 1912.
Estimate of the Montessori System of Child Training. L. A. Williams.

Pedagogical Seminary, Vol. 18, pp. 533–543, December 1911.
Dr. Montessori and Her Houses of Childhood. Dr. T. L. Smith.
Primary Plans, Vol. 10, pp. 9–10, 39–40, November 1912.
Montessori Method, Self-Education. Mrs. H. H. Bullock.
Popular Educator, Vol. 30, pp. 311–313. February 1913.
The Newest Educational Enthusiasm. M. V. O'Shea.
Primary Education, Vol. 20, pp. 313–316, June 1912.
The Montessori Method and Primary Education. Ellen Yale
Stevens.
School Journal, Vol. 80, pp. 135–136, February 1913.
The Montessori Method in Relation to the Rural Schools.
Myron T. Scudder.
Scientific American, Vol. 106, pp. 564–565, June 22, 1912.
What is the Montessori Method? S. M. Gruenberg.
An unprejudiced view of the method and some hints for its
adaptation. The article is illustrated with photographs of
Miss George's Montessori school in Washington.
Survey, Vol. 27, pp. 1595–1597, June 20, 1912.
The Montessori Method of Educating Children. R. R. Reeder.
Technical World, April 1913.
Shocked into Smartness. F. G. Moorehead.
Volte Review offers the following articles:
Vol. 14, pp. 48–49, 74–85, April, May 1912.
The Montessori Method and the Deaf Child.
Vol. 14, pp. 146–147, June 1912.
The Montessori Method Applicable to the Deaf. Mme.
Margueles.
Vol. 14, pp. 154–168.
The Montessori Method of Teaching Hearing Children. Mrs.
J. Scott Anderson.
Woman's Home Companion began a series of articles September
1913. These are written by Mary Heaton Vorse and dis-
cuss the Montessori principle and the American mother
at home. The writer has visited the Italian schools.

INDEX

Arithmetic, 138.
    American methods in, 138–139.
    Definite number work, 120–135.
    Fundamental processes, 125–134.
    Indefinite comparison, 118–120.
    Metric system, 135.
    Number content, 138.
    Pestalozzi, Froebel, Spear, Dewey, theories of, 138–139.
Ayres', discussion of remedial measures, 224.

Barnes, on sense training, 87 ; on social capacity, 182.

Casa dei Bambini,
    Cloister School, 10.
    Compared with the kindergarten, 203–208.
    Directress of, 36–38.
    Establishment of, 7.
    Freedom in, 13–15.
    Impressions of, 15.
    Pincian Hill School, 11.
    Program for, 23–24.
    Requirements for entrance, 8.
Child study movement, 32, 33.
Child, teacher, and curriculum, 200, 208.
Child training, Aristotle's three conditions for, 184.
Children, abnormal, brought up to grade, 6.
Children, defective conditions in, 4, 5, 53, 55.
Children, responsibility in rearing, 168.
Chubb, on language arts, 107.
Clay, the value of, 154–155.
Collective interest, 29.
Color, 75, 82.
Color, matching, 21.
Composition, 107–110.
Comradeship, love of, 23.
Constructive motive, 145–148.

Design, 93, 94, 155.
Dewey, 211.
Didactic material,
    Alphabets, 21.
    Broad stair, 20, 72, 118.
    Chest of drawers for textures, 18, 69.
    Color tablets, 75.
    Conditions desirable for the use of, 85, 86.
    Cylindrical insets, 18, 72, 74.
    Demonstration and use of, 177.
    Frames for lacing, etc., 10.
    How presented, 83.
    Insets for making designs, 21.
    In the home, 174–180.
    In the Montessori school, 17–33.
    Long stair, 20, 70.
    Plane geometric forms, 75.
    Plane geometric insets, 74.
    Sandpaper board, 36; figures, 124; letters, 100, 101.
    Sound boxes, 76.
    Tablets for weighing, 71.
    Tower, 24, 72.
    Typical exercises with, 78–85.
    Writing table, 93.
Discipline, how obtained, 33–35, 41–47.
Drawing, 155–160.

Elementary school, history of, 191.
Environment, 29, 57, 59.

Fisher, Dorothy Canfield, 40, 80, 81.
Formal sense training, 87.
Freedom, 28, 31, 33.
Free-hand drawing, 158.
Froebel, 32, 37, 65.

Games, 22.
Gesell, on touch, 62, 63, 67.
Good Building Association of Rome, 7.

R   241

AMERICAN EDUCATION:
ITS MEN, IDEAS, AND INSTITUTIONS
An Arno Press/New York Times Collection

Series I

Adams, Francis. **The Free School System of the United States.** 1875.

Alcott, William A. **Confessions of a School Master.** 1839.

American Unitarian Association. **From Servitude to Service.** 1905.

Bagley, William C. **Determinism in Education.** 1925.

Barnard, Henry, editor. **Memoirs of Teachers, Educators, and Promoters and Benefactors of Education, Literature, and Science.** 1861.

Bell, Sadie. **The Church, the State, and Education in Virginia.** 1930.

Belting, Paul Everett. **The Development of the Free Public High School in Illinois to 1860.** 1919.

Berkson, Isaac B. **Theories of Americanization: A Critical Study.** 1920.

Blauch, Lloyd E. **Federal Cooperation in Agricultural Extension Work, Vocational Education, and Vocational Rehabilitation.** 1935.

Bloomfield, Meyer. **Vocational Guidance of Youth.** 1911.

Brewer, Clifton Hartwell. **A History of Religious Education in the Episcopal Church to 1835.** 1924.

Brown, Elmer Ellsworth. **The Making of Our Middle Schools.** 1902.

Brumbaugh, M. G. **Life and Works of Christopher Dock.** 1908.

Burns, Reverend J. A. **The Catholic School System in the United States.** 1908.

Burns, Reverend J. A. **The Growth and Development of the Catholic School System in the United States.** 1912.

Burton, Warren. **The District School as It Was.** 1850.

Butler, Nicholas Murray, editor. **Education in the United States.** 1900.

Butler, Vera M. **Education as Revealed By New England Newspapers prior to 1850.** 1935.

Campbell, Thomas Monroe. **The Movable School Goes to the Negro Farmer.** 1936.

Carter, James G. **Essays upon Popular Education.** 1826.

Carter, James G. **Letters to the Hon. William Prescott, LL.D., on the Free Schools of New England.** 1824.

Channing, William Ellery. **Self-Culture.** 1842.

Coe, George A. **A Social Theory of Religious Education.** 1917.

Committee on Secondary School Studies. **Report of the Committee on Secondary School Studies, Appointed at the Meeting of the National Education Association.** 1893.

Counts, George S. **Dare the School Build a New Social Order?** 1932.

Counts, George S. **The Selective Character of American Secondary Education.** 1922.

Counts, George S. **The Social Composition of Boards of Education.** 1927.

Culver, Raymond B. **Horace Mann and Religion in the Massachusetts Public Schools.** 1929.

Curoe, Philip R. V. **Educational Attitudes and Policies of Organized Labor in the United States.** 1926.

Dabney, Charles William. **Universal Education in the South.** 1936.

Dearborn, Ned Harland. **The Oswego Movement in American Education.** 1925.

De Lima, Agnes. **Our Enemy the Child.** 1926.

Dewey, John. **The Educational Situation.** 1902.

Dexter, Franklin B., editor. **Documentary History of Yale University.** 1916.

Eliot, Charles William. **Educational Reform: Essays and Addresses.** 1898.

Ensign, Forest Chester. **Compulsory School Attendance and Child Labor.** 1921.

Fitzpatrick, Edward Augustus. **The Educational Views and Influence of De Witt Clinton.** 1911.

Fleming, Sanford. **Children & Puritanism.** 1933.

Flexner, Abraham. **The American College: A Criticism.** 1908.

Foerster, Norman. **The Future of the Liberal College.** 1938.

Gilman, Daniel Coit. **University Problems in the United States.** 1898.

Hall, Samuel R. **Lectures on School-Keeping.** 1829.

Hall, Stanley G. **Adolescence: Its Psychology and Its Relations to Physiology, Anthropology, Sociology, Sex, Crime, Religion, and Education.** 1905. 2 vols.

Hansen, Allen Oscar. **Early Educational Leadership in the Ohio Valley.** 1923.

Harris, William T. **Psychologic Foundations of Education.** 1899.

Harris, William T. **Report of the Committee of Fifteen on the Elementary School.** 1895.

Harveson, Mae Elizabeth. **Catharine Esther Beecher: Pioneer Educator.** 1932.

Jackson, George Leroy. **The Development of School Support in Colonial Massachusetts.** 1909.

Kandel, I. L., editor. **Twenty-five Years of American Education.** 1924.

Kemp, William Webb. **The Support of Schools in Colonial New York by the Society for the Propagation of the Gospel in Foreign Parts.** 1913.

Kilpatrick, William Heard. **The Dutch Schools of New Netherland and Colonial New York.** 1912.

Kilpatrick, William Heard. **The Educational Frontier.** 1933.

Knight, Edgar Wallace. **The Influence of Reconstruction on Education in the South.** 1913.

Le Duc, Thomas. **Piety and Intellect at Amherst College, 1865-1912.** 1946.

Maclean, John. **History of the College of New Jersey from Its Origin in 1746 to the Commencement of 1854.** 1877.

Maddox, William Arthur. **The Free School Idea in Virginia before the Civil War.** 1918.

Mann, Horace. **Lectures on Education.** 1855.

McCadden, Joseph J. **Education in Pennsylvania, 1801-1835, and Its Debt to Roberts Vaux.** 1855.

McCallum, James Dow. **Eleazar Wheelock.** 1939.

McCuskey, Dorothy. **Bronson Alcott, Teacher.** 1940.

Meiklejohn, Alexander. **The Liberal College.** 1920.

Miller, Edward Alanson. **The History of Educational Legislation in Ohio from 1803 to 1850.** 1918.

Miller, George Frederick. The Academy System of the State of New York. 1922.
Monroe, Will S. History of the Pestalozzian Movement in the United States. 1907.
Mosely Education Commission. Reports of the Mosely Education Commission to the United States of America October-December, 1903. 1904.
Mowry, William A. Recollections of a New England Educator. 1908.
Mulhern, James. A History of Secondary Education in Pennsylvania. 1933.
National Herbart Society. National Herbart Society Yearbooks 1-5, 1895-1899. 1895-1899.
Nearing, Scott. The New Education: A Review of Progressive Educational Movements of the Day. 1915.
Neef, Joseph. Sketches of a Plan and Method of Education. 1808.
Nock, Albert Jay. The Theory of Education in the United States. 1932.
Norton, A. O., editor. The First State Normal School in America: The Journals of Cyrus Pierce and Mary Swift. 1926.
Oviatt, Edwin. The Beginnings of Yale, 1701-1726. 1916.
Packard, Frederic Adolphus. The Daily Public School in the United States. 1866.
Page, David P. Theory and Practice of Teaching. 1848.
Parker, Francis W. Talks on Pedagogics: An Outline of the Theory of Concentration. 1894.
Peabody, Elizabeth Palmer. Record of a School. 1835.
Porter, Noah. The American Colleges and the American Public. 1870.
Reigart, John Franklin. The Lancasterian System of Instruction in the Schools of New York City. 1916.
Reilly, Daniel F. The School Controversy (1891-1893). 1943.
Rice, Dr. J. M. The Public-School System of the United States. 1893.
Rice, Dr. J. M. Scientific Management in Education. 1912.
Ross, Early D. Democracy's College: The Land-Grant Movement in the Formative Stage. 1942.
Rugg, Harold, et al. Curriculum-Making: Past and Present. 1926.
Rugg, Harold, et al. The Foundations of Curriculum-Making. 1926.
Rugg, Harold and Shumaker, Ann. The Child-Centered School. 1928.
Seybolt, Robert Francis. Apprenticeship and Apprenticeship Education in Colonial New England and New York. 1917.
Seybolt, Robert Francis. The Private Schools of Colonial Boston. 1935.
Seybolt, Robert Francis. The Public Schools of Colonial Boston. 1935.
Sheldon, Henry D. Student Life and Customs. 1901.
Sherrill, Lewis Joseph. Presbyterian Parochial Schools, 1846-1870. 1932 .
Siljestrom, P. A. Educational Institutions of the United States. 1853.
Small, Walter Herbert. Early New England Schools. 1914.
Soltes, Mordecai. The Yiddish Press: An Americanizing Agency. 1925.
Stewart, George, Jr. A History of Religious Education in Connecticut to the Middle of the Nineteenth Century. 1924.
Storr, Richard J. The Beginnings of Graduate Education in America. 1953.

Stout, John Elbert. **The Development of High-School Curricula in the North Central States from 1860 to 1918.** 1921.
Suzzallo, Henry. **The Rise of Local School Supervision in Massachusetts.** 1906.
Swett, John. **Public Education in California.** 1911.
Tappan, Henry P. **University Education.** 1851.
Taylor, Howard Cromwell. **The Educational Significance of the Early Federal Land Ordinances.** 1921.
Taylor, J. Orville. **The District School.** 1834.
Tewksbury, Donald G. **The Founding of American Colleges and Universities before the Civil War.** 1932.
Thorndike, Edward L. **Educational Psychology.** 1913-1914.
True, Alfred Charles. **A History of Agricultural Education in the United States, 1785-1925.** 1929.
True, Alfred Charles. **A History of Agricultural Extension Work in the United States, 1785-1923.** 1928.
Updegraff, Harlan. **The Origin of the Moving School in Massachusetts.** 1908.
Wayland, Francis. **Thoughts on the Present Collegiate System in the United States.** 1842.
Weber, Samuel Edwin. **The Charity School Movement in Colonial Pennsylvania.** 1905.
Wells, Guy Fred. **Parish Education in Colonial Virginia.** 1923.
Wickersham, J. P. **The History of Education in Pennsylvania.** 1885.
Woodward, Calvin M. **The Manual Training School.** 1887.
Woody, Thomas. **Early Quaker Education in Pennsylvania.** 1920.
Woody, Thomas. **Quaker Education in the Colony and State of New Jersey.** 1923.
Wroth, Lawrence C. **An American Bookshelf, 1755.** 1934.

Series II

Adams, Evelyn C. **American Indian Education.** 1946.
Bailey, Joseph Cannon. **Seaman A. Knapp: Schoolmaster of American Agriculture.** 1945.
Beecher, Catharine and Harriet Beecher Stowe. **The American Woman's Home.** 1869.
Benezet, Louis T. **General Education in the Progressive College.** 1943.
Boas, Louise Schutz. **Woman's Education Begins.** 1935.
Bobbitt, Franklin. **The Curriculum.** 1918.
Bode, Boyd H. **Progressive Education at the Crossroads.** 1938.
Bourne, William Oland. **History of the Public School Society of the City of New York.** 1870.
Bronson, Walter C. **The History of Brown University, 1764-1914.** 1914.
Burstall, Sara A. **The Education of Girls in the United States.** 1894.
Butts, R. Freeman. **The College Charts Its Course.** 1939.
Caldwell, Otis W. and Stuart A. Courtis. **Then & Now in Education, 1845-1923.** 1923.
Calverton, V. F. & Samuel D. Schmalhausen, editors. **The New Generation: The Intimate Problems of Modern Parents and Children.** 1930.
Charters, W. W. **Curriculum Construction.** 1923.
Childs, John L. **Education and Morals.** 1950.

Childs, John L. Education and the Philosophy of Experimentalism. 1931.
Clapp, Elsie Ripley. Community Schools in Action. 1939.
Counts, George S. The American Road to Culture: A Social Interpretation of Education in the United States. 1930.
Counts, George S. School and Society in Chicago. 1928.
Finegan, Thomas E. Free Schools. 1921.
Fletcher, Robert Samuel. A History of Oberlin College. 1943.
Grattan, C. Hartley. In Quest of Knowledge: A Historical Perspective on Adult Education. 1955.
Hartman, Gertrude & Ann Shumaker, editors. Creative Expression. 1932.
Kandel, I. L. The Cult of Uncertainty. 1943.
Kandel, I. L. Examinations and Their Substitutes in the United States. 1936.
Kilpatrick, William Heard. Education for a Changing Civilization. 1926.
Kilpatrick, William Heard. Foundations of Method. 1925.
Kilpatrick, William Heard. The Montessori System Examined. 1914.
Lang, Ossian H., editor. Educational Creeds of the Nineteenth Century. 1898.
Learned, William S. The Quality of the Educational Process in the United States and in Europe. 1927.
Meiklejohn, Alexander. The Experimental College. 1932.
Middlekauff, Robert. Ancients and Axioms: Secondary Education in Eighteenth-Century New England. 1963.
Norwood, William Frederick. Medical Education in the United States Before the Civil War. 1944.
Parsons, Elsie W. Clews. Educational Legislation and Administration of the Colonial Governments. 1899.
Perry, Charles M. Henry Philip Tappan: Philosopher and University President. 1933.
Pierce, Bessie Louise. Civic Attitudes in American School Textbooks. 1930.
Rice, Edwin Wilbur. The Sunday-School Movement (1780-1917) and the American Sunday-School Union (1817-1917). 1917.
Robinson, James Harvey. The Humanizing of Knowledge. 1924.
Ryan, W. Carson. Studies in Early Graduate Education. 1939.
Seybolt, Robert Francis. The Evening School in Colonial America. 1925.
Seybolt, Robert Francis. Source Studies in American Colonial Education. 1925.
Todd, Lewis Paul. Wartime Relations of the Federal Government and the Public Schools, 1917-1918. 1945.
Vandewalker, Nina C. The Kindergarten in American Education. 1908.
Ward, Florence Elizabeth. The Montessori Method and the American School. 1913.
West, Andrew Fleming. Short Papers on American Liberal Education. 1907.
Wright, Marion M. Thompson. The Education of Negroes in New Jersey. 1941.

Supplement

The Social Frontier (Frontiers of Democracy). Vols. 1-10, 1934-1943.